"*Regardless of the business you are in, people who come to work fully engaged and firing on all cylinders are your major point of differentiation. Why? Inspiring impassioned people is the hardest thing to get right. It's also the hardest thing for your competitors to replicate. Loaded with great stories and backed with irrefutable research, Stark and Flaherty deliver <u>the</u> blueprint for creating a culture where people want to work and choose to stay!*"
—Dr. Kevin Freiberg, author of *Boom!*, *Guts!*, and *Nuts!*

"*It's a compelling read with turn-key 'do it now' suggestions that I can put into practice today.*" —Chris Folz, vice president, human resources, Wells Fargo

"*If your company has any employees, this book is a must read. Peter and Jane cut to the bottom line in the very complicated, and sometimes messy, arena of employee opinion surveys and the leaders who have the courage to ask.*"
—Michael Easley, CEO, Powder River Energy Corporation

"*Once again, Stark and Flaherty have qualified and quantified the how's and why's of creating an environment in which associates are passionate, and are energized to contribute discretionary efforts to make an organization a success. Quite frankly, you're doing your business a disservice by not embracing the concepts.*" —Paul Barnes, president, SheaHomes, San Diego Division

"*Engaged! offers strategies that are critical to increasing organizational excellence, especially in these turbulent times. If you want to energize your employees so they are giving their best work to you and your customers then this book is mandatory reading.*"
—Jon Peters, president, The Institute for Management Studies

"*This timely book puts the focus on what the Best-of-the-Best leaders actually do to make a difference. [Engaged!] risks sharing what works and what doesn't work…. Don't just read it—devour it!*"
—Terry Paulson, PhD, professional speaker and president, Paulson and Associates, Inc.

"*Great information, quick and easy to read. Very frank and to the point. Employee engagement is the key of any organization—most organizations know that. But what they don't know is how to get there. What does employee engagement look like in the workplace, and what specific things can be done to create that culture? This book addresses that specifically with lots of practical things to do to get there.*"
—Pam Smith, deputy director, San Diego County Health & Human Service

"*This book has it all—simple, straightforward, and actionable!*"
—Sadie Stern, director of human resources, LG Electronics

"Anyone who leads a world-class organization or who is trying to create a world-class organization should not only read Engaged! but should put its practical advice to work. The strategies in the book are relatively easy to implement and can create huge impact. Engaged! provides many great ideas that will move your organization to the front of the pack."

—Doran Barnes, CEO, Foothill Transit

"The authors have drawn from years of experience working intimately with leaders and organizations to set forth a helpful guide for leaders. The book helps one take stock of one's own leadership and organization and the do's and don'ts of building a productive culture where employees not only enjoy their work, but produce at high levels. I found the practical and down-to-earth strategies extremely helpful as I continue to strive to become an even more effective leader."   —Don Phillips, superintendent, Poway Unified School District

"Great book. Quick reading with ideas on ways to improve the way employees feel about their company." —Bruce Hendricks, president and CEO, Bank of Nevada

"Engaged! is a must read for all CEOs, upper-level, mid-level, and new managers who aspire to become great leaders. Recognizing that your company's greatest assets are its people is the first step, but recognition is not enough. This book will give you the tool set to develop your leadership skills to their full potential and help you create a management team and work culture that is productive, customer friendly, and will have your people whistling as they are driving to work on Monday morning."

—Timothy Fennell, CEO/GM, Del Mar Fairgrounds/Racetrack

"Organizational change is all about first changing behaviors and ultimately attitudes of your employees. This book moves to the heart of attitudinal change."   —Lowell Billings, superintendent, Chula Vista Elementary School District

"This book is a very informative document that enables managers to learn how to be leaders who engage their employees and create the employer of choice."

—Gail Sullivan, Deputy City Manager, City of Escondido

"For many senior people it is not so much that we need to be taught as we need to be reminded about these items. But, for many relatively new to management roles it may be their initial exposure and the need is real. Have them all read this book."   —Jim Konrath, retired chairman and CEO, Accredited Home Lenders

ENGAGED!

HOW LEADERS BUILD ORGANIZATIONS WHERE EMPLOYEES LOVE TO COME TO WORK

PETER B. STARK & JANE FLAHERTY

PETER BARRON STARK COMPANIES • SAN DIEGO

PUBLISHED BY BENTLEY PRESS, INC.

Peter Barron Stark Companies
11417 W. Bernardo Ct.
San Diego, CA 92127-1639
1.877.727.6468
1.858.451.3601
http://www.pbsconsulting.com
http://www.employeeopinionsurveys.com
http://www.peterstark.com

Designed by Debbie Glasserman

Edited by Pat Ryan, Susan Suffes, and Jessica Swift

First, we dedicate this book to our clients. You are the leaders who partner with us to conduct employee opinion surveys. Then you use the results to create environments where employees love to come to work and customers love to do business. Your engaged employees look forward to going to work, will give their discretionary effort, and will go to the wall to ensure that you, and your organization, are successful. You truly make a significant difference to your employees and customers. We thank you!

Second, we dedicate this book to all the bosses who do not see a need to listen to their employee's feedback or act on their opinions—much less continuously strive to improve their departments and organizations. As one senior manager told us when we tried to explain the value of an employee opinion survey, "I already know what the employees think and I don't plan on changing if I learn something new." It is these managers who lose touch with reality, don't even know they have lost touch with reality, and unknowingly produce poor working environments. It is this group of managers who make the leaders listed above look like heroes. When their environment turns sour enough—measured by a lack of productivity, teamwork, communication, quality, service, and profitability—these managers willingly turn to us for help. We thank you, too.

Finally, on October 21, 2006, Joe Prandini, the CEO and general manager of Betteravia Farms, one of the largest farmers and packers of produce in the United States, passed away. For fifteen years we have partnered with Betteravia and seen firsthand the power of Joe's great leadership. A true gift to the spirit, Joe possessed a compelling and positive vision for his organization's future. He built strong, caring relationships that led people to enthusiastically follow him to achieve the shared vision. When we talked to Joe about what the great organizations we worked with were doing to create workplace excellence, Joe used to say, "That is really powerful stuff. You ought to write about it." All who knew Joe will miss him. Joe, this book is also for you.

CONTENTS

If you desire to be the type of leader who creates an environment where your employees love to come to work and your customers love doing business, *Engaged!* is the book for you. For the past twenty years, we at Peter Barron Stark Companies have taken great pride in being a leading management consulting firm that works with all types of organizations to build a great work environment. During this time we have conducted over 250 different organizational assessments and gathered and analyzed the opinions of over 100,000 managers and employees from hundreds of organizations around the world. We have interpreted the opinions of these people and provided hard data to leaders in banking, manufacturing, high-tech, healthcare, pharmaceutical, professional sports, law, retail, food service, and many other diverse industries.

When we're asked what employees think about their jobs, organizations, immediate supervisors, and management, we can answer the question with confidence. We know the secrets of the Best-of-the-Best organizations. We see what their leaders do to engage employees.

In *Engaged!* you will learn about the ten key attributes that differentiate the Best-of-the-Best organizations (those in the top quartile) from the other three-quarters of the companies that comprise the rest of the pack. You will read about the eleven stupid things managers do to undermine workplace excellence, and what can be done to recover from those mistakes and move into a positive leadership role. We'll share the techniques that leaders can use to single-handedly make a difference, even in the most difficult situations. Finally, we'll give you seventy-six strategies to achieve workplace excellence. We have watched our clients use them and have measured their success. We know these strategies work!

If you are a leader who is focused on the future and understands that you can't reach your full leadership potential without the commitment and loyalty of engaged employees, read on. Because the truth is this: *If people do not willingly follow you, you will be a manager but not a leader.*

Whether you feel members of your team walk on water or are just barely keeping their heads above the waves, our findings will convince you that knowing what your employees think, and knowing the most important actions to take to create workplace excellence, are absolutely critical to ensure your success as a leader.

THE WINNING NUMBERS: BENCHMARKING THE BEST IN CLASS

Our expertise is understanding your workforce. We partner with clients to help them identify and implement best practices and figure out how to achieve optimum results through a powerful team. Our goal is to make you an employer of choice. That means the best people will want to work for you and contribute to your organization's goals. With a contracting workforce and expanding competition, that's a worthy goal.

So you need a starting point, a benchmark, to find out how your employees view their workplace and your management team. After all, you can't improve if you don't know your areas of strength, much less your areas of weakness.

Benchmarking is a valuable tool that allows you to compare the results of your survey against the results of other organizations. You know the approach. A group of companies measures key indicators for success. The indicators are reported and aggregated and the benchmark numbers are produced. Using the scale, the top-performing companies become the best in class.

We utilize two separate benchmarks to guide our clients' successes in building workplace excellence: the Overall Benchmark of all companies, and the Best-of-the-Best Benchmark that isolates the top 25 percent (highest-rated) organizations surveyed.

Remember all those industries we have surveyed? Because of our wide reach across diverse fields, our benchmarks are broadly representative of the attitudes and opinions of many employees. The survey results also capture the management practices of good-to-great companies. We can say this with confidence because companies that do not place much value on employee satisfaction do not conduct surveys. It is highly unlikely they can achieve the status of a good-to-great employer.

An employee opinion survey provides the objective data you need to identify employee attitudes and take action to become an employer of choice. More than that, you will surround yourself with satisfied team members who are engaged in their work, creative with solutions, and generally pleasant to be around. That's how you spend your time and your energy on being a leader who produces results.

After collecting data from thousands of employees, consistent response patterns pinpointed the areas where the Best-of-the-Best excel. Using the survey data and the themes that emerged from personal interviews with employees and managers, we identified the key areas that differentiated these leading organizations from those in the Overall Benchmark.

WHAT MAKES THE BEST-OF-THE-BEST THE BEST?

What are the trendsetters doing to achieve superior results? In the years we have been conducting employee opinion surveys, the bar is continually being raised for the Best-of-the-Best Benchmark. Currently, at a minimum, an organization needs to have an overall favorable response rate of 82 percent to make the cut and be considered among the Best-of-the-Best.

Our surveys measure employee engagement and satisfaction in what we call "percent favorable," which combines the percent of "strongly agree" plus "agree" responses. For employee opinion surveys, we are more concerned with whether employees are in agreement with statements in the survey (strongly agree and agree) than we are with the strength of the agreement. For example, in reviewing the responses to the following statement: "Senior management has clearly communicated the company's strategic direction to me." 83.8 percent of all survey respondents strongly agreed or agreed.

There are one hundred questions in the majority of surveys we conduct. Out of these one hundred questions, the results often show a substantial difference between companies in the Best-of-the-Best Benchmark and those in the Overall Benchmark. You'll see the differences when you read "The 10 Keys to Workplace Excellence" section in chapter two.

The difference between the favorable ratings in the Overall Benchmark and the ratings in the Best-of-the-Best Benchmark in these ten key areas ranged from 9.7 to 29.3 percentage points, and averaged 14 points difference per question between the two benchmarks.

Over time, as we presented survey data to our clients, they asked us, "Are our results good?" and "How do we compare to the best organizations?" You will find the answers to these questions in the following chapters.

We will review the benchmark data, identify what the Best-of-the-Best companies do compared with others, and add in our analysis of the best practices. The result will give you the tools you need to join the leaders in the Best-of-the-Best Benchmark.

HOW WE CAN HELP YOU SUCCEED

If you were a client, here is what we would do.

To identify areas of strength and deficit, we would design a customized employee opinion survey for distribution to managers and employees. They rate their perceptions of the support they get to do their best work, which provides the quantitative data. The results of their employee opinion survey are often a revelation for many organizations.

> **TIP**
>
> **How does your workplace stack up to the Best-of-the-Best? Take the test: Go to www.peterstark.com, and enter the word ENGAGE in the Tip Box.**

Then we would conduct in-person interviews with both line employees and managers to obtain qualitative information. With their input, we could discover the major issues affecting the company's employee performance and, therefore, the company's performance.

Finally, based on the results of the survey and the interviews, we would help you improve your company's support of employees and, concurrently, your employees' support of customers. By implementing action plans and utilizing executive coaching strategies, we would help your managers become even better leaders and your organizations to achieve their goals.

What is the situation at your company? Maybe there is an employees-related problem to solve. Or perhaps you want to know how the best companies take care of their workers. Maybe you realize that to rise to the next level in your career, you need to improve your team's performance.

You've come to the right place. We're going to share with you the benchmark data along with the insights gained from two decades of interviewing and coaching leaders. You'll learn what employees think about the best managers and their organizations. Most importantly, you'll see what you can do to become a respected leader who produces results.

PART ONE

The Case for Workplace Excellence

1

Become the Employer of Choice

The bottom line rules business. If you want to generate more profit, you need employees who are engaged with their jobs. Why? Motivated to improve your product and your service, they want to come to work. Even better, their positive attitude is contagious. These workers achieve results, which earns money for your company. Furthermore, they want to stay with you because they feel fulfilled in their work. You are their employer of choice.

Employees with an above-average attitude toward their work will generate higher customer satisfaction, higher productivity, and higher profits for their organizations.

In addition, companies with higher morale (more than 70%) outperformed those in the same industries by 11.3% (data compiled by *The Enthusiastic Employee* and published by the Wharton School of Business). It's clear that maintaining a vital, engaged workforce has a significant impact on the bottom line.

WORKFORCE WOES

As we write this, the economy is in a downturn and many employees with concerns about layoffs might be doing their best in order to save their jobs.

However, when the economy improves, employment choices in many industries will be plentiful. But engaged employees are less likely to look for other employment opportunities and walk away with all the training and experience you've provided.

And that is important to remember because the cost of replacing an employee is staggering. Most human resource professionals estimate a cost of between 70% and 200% of an employee's annual salary to replace lost talent. Dealing with low morale is a time-consuming headache. Why do it when you don't have to?

An employer of choice measures employee engagement and satis-faction and takes action to address key areas of concern. When employees know you listen, care, and will respond to their feedback, they will choose you.

Here is something else to keep in mind: There will be a worker shortage in the future. While the statistics vary, all current research projects a shrinking workforce. How will you compete if you can't hire and retain high-quality workers? Perhaps an even bigger price is paid by the brain drain that occurs when employees leave and take their knowledge and training with them. Employee attrition costs you personally in the effort to hire and train, and it costs your team members as they first compensate for a missing position, then spend time training the new recruit.

Consider that 55% of employees plan to quit, or think often of quitting, when the job market in their geographic location regains strength (Sibson and Company). Or that *up to 41% of your workforce* is already looking to take their experience—and a piece of your company culture—to another employer or, even worse, to a direct competitor (WorkTrends, Gantz Wiley Research).

If you are confident that you can rely on direct supervisors to take care of turnover issues, the following fact may change your outlook: a study by Accenture found that 63% of mid-level managers are readying their resumes, just waiting for the job market to strengthen.

An employee's plan to leave your company "when the job market strengthens" is a serious concern. In a 2006 survey of 451 human resources professionals and 300 managerial and executive staff, over 56% agreed that employee turnover will rise significantly once the job market improves (Society of Human Resource Management).

Then there are the demographics. In 2006, baby boomers (approximately 76 million people born between 1946 and 1964) began to turn 60. In the year 2000, workers ages 55 and older accounted for 12.9% of our workforce. According to the U.S. Department of Labor, by 2015 they will make up approximately 20% of the workforce. Then they'll retire.

Baby boomers leaving the workplace is significant not only because of the skill sets they take with them, but because of the decline in the birth rate of successive generations. There are fewer Generation Xers, Generation Yers, and Millenials to take their places. Looking into the future, the U.S. Bureau of Labor Statistics estimates a shortage of 10 million workers in the U.S. by 2010.

WATCH EMPLOYEES LEAVE

When we asked employees why they begin searching for a new job, the following responses were given most frequently:

- The supervisor or manager does not value the employee's contribution or appear to care about the employee.
- The supervisor does not provide good, ongoing communication to the employee.
- The supervisor does not provide the employee with performance feedback.
- The supervisor is late on the performance appraisal.
- The supervisor treats the employee disrespectfully.
- The supervisor fails to provide the employee with clear direction.

- The employee feels there is little potential for career development.
- The employee is ready for a more challenging position or a new experience.
- The employee seeks better compensation and benefits.

> **In most instances, people leave because they lack a meaningful working relationship with an immediate supervisor.**

Many of these reasons are within the manager's control, yet when we interview managers and ask why their people departed for another organization, the most frequent response given is a higher salary. Most times the managers state that they had no hope of keeping the employee from jumping ship because they had no control over matching the employee's higher salary offer.

When we interview employees who leave, it's a different story. Most employees who leave organizations do receive a higher salary. But the amount of the increase is surprising—the average salary increase is approximately 6%. Ask yourself this question: If you loved your job and your boss really valued your contributions, would you risk all that to go to work for another organization for just a 6% increase in salary?

When employees answer this question, most think about it for a moment and then say, "No." But, what if you did not love your job and you had a bad boss? In this situation, a 6% increase in salary would seem like an opportunity you would not want to pass up.

In most instances, people leave because they lack a meaningful working relationship with an immediate supervisor. It's not the money. The stronger this relationship is, the lesser role money will play when an employee considers leaving the company for a competing offer.

THE EMPLOYEE WHO ISN'T THERE

There may be fifty ways to leave your lover, but there are only two ways employees leave an organization. Sometimes it is physically, as in moving on to a competitor, which is manageable; at least you know the employee is no longer on your team. You are clear on the next step—hire a great employee to take over the job.

The second way is the one that strikes fear into the heart of every manager: the employee who mentally quits, but stays with the organization. There are five warning signs to help you determine your employees' level of engagement and give you a "heads up" that an employee has mentally resigned. They are:

- **Evidence of a "whatever" attitude.** The employee is not confrontational, but clearly is not motivated.
- **Minimal contribution that produces a mediocre level of performance.** The employee shows up right on time, leaves right on time, and does just enough to keep his/her job, and no more.
- **Absenteeism.** The employee uses up all sick, vacation, or PTO (personal time off) time on a regular basis.
- **Loss of enthusiasm.** The employee may have been a motivated contributor but now withdraws and contributes little.
- **Little or no interest in the future.** Whether you are discussing a vision for the future or your office holiday party, this employee is clearly only interested in what's "here and now."

CONTENTED COWS GIVE BETTER MILK

As Bill Catlette and Richard Hadden shared in their book, *Contented Cows Give Better Milk*, organizations that don't measure up in the eyes of their employees tend to be viewed as an employer of last resort. Either the organization is forced to pay market-premium wages and salaries in an attempt to secure better applicants, or it must accept lower-quality applicants—or both.

In their research on contented organizations, Catlette and Hadden compared the growth, revenue, and net job gain (generation of new jobs) of six Contented Organizations with that of six Common Organizations in similar industries. To make the Contented Cow list, organizations were required to meet the following minimum criteria:

- Profitability—a consistent track record of growth in revenue and earnings
- Continuity—in business for at least five years
- Desirability—generally regarded by the people who work within the organization as a good place to work, with positive employee relations' practices

Their research showed that the Contented Organizations outgrew the Common Organizations by a four-to-one margin, outearned them by nearly $40 billion, and generated a net difference of better than 800,000 jobs. Catlette and Hadden also found that the Contented Organizations were remarkably similar in three areas:

- Aligning their people with their organization's purpose and objectives
- Caring about and recognizing people
- Enabling people to perform by providing necessary training, information, and tools

In our Peter Barron Companies research we see it over and over: Successful organizations separate themselves from less-prosperous organizations by providing employees with an understanding of the company's mission and vision, setting clear expectations, helping people understand the significance of their contributions to the company, and giving them the opportunity to learn and grow.

Our findings prove that the extent to which people do or do not fully contribute is governed more by attitude than by necessity, fear, or economic influence. If you want to be an employer of choice—and a business success—it's all in your organization's attitude. And that *attitude* can be best realized by following the 10 Keys to Workplace Excellence.

2

The 10 Keys to Workplace Excellence

Amazing as it may sound, there are only ten keys that distinguish Best-of-the-Best organizations. Using them allows you entrance into the exclusive territory of employer of *first* choice. They are:

1. A Compelling, Positive Vision with Clear Goals
2. Communication—The Right Stuff at the Right Time
3. Select the Right People for the Right Job
4. Remember, We're on the Same Team
5. Cool Stuff—Continuous Improvement and Innovation
6. Recognize and Reward Excellent Performance
7. Accountability Counts
8. Every Employee Learns and Grows
9. Problems . . . No Problem!
10. It's All About the Customer

These ten keys give the Best-of-the-Best organizations a distinct competitive advantage in the market: Because of their particular relationship with management and the organization, their employees are willing to expend a discretionary effort. Basically, because the employees "get" more, they "give" more. It's not unusual for an employee opinion survey to show an overall, company-wide favorable response of 78%. Yet surprisingly, there is often a variance of thirty to fifty percentage points between managers.

Each key is under the direct control of an employee's immediate manager or supervisor. That means you—and the people you coach— can change the way you lead to improve performance.

There are two ways to improve the results of an employee opinion survey. First, the manager can change and exhibit new leadership behaviors. Second, senior management can make a tough decision and change the manager of the area that has low results. Sometimes the leadership change improves the organization, but other times one leader leaving the organization can have a devastating impact on workplace excellence.

> People join an organization for a job and leave because of a manager.

As a leader, do not ever underestimate your role, power, and responsibility to create an environment where your employees love to come to work and your customers love to do business. You can make a meaningful difference to your direct reports and your organization, in spite of decisions made by senior management or even the board. The old cliché is supported by our research: People join an organization for a job and leave because of a manager.

If you are a manager who wants to make a significant contribution in your organization and in the lives of your employees, use the ten keys to focus your leadership. These keys are the result of nearly twenty years of research and they reflect our expertise in coaching managers to improve the environment for their employees.

Key #1: A Compelling, Positive Vision with Clear Goals

There is no doubt that one of the great management buzzwords of our time is *vision*. It is high on the list with other words like *stakeholders* and *paradigm*. A clear mental image of a desired future outcome, a vision is like the picture on a jigsaw puzzle box that shows you exactly what you are trying to create. Call it a vision, mission, purpose, philosophy, or values—the labels vary—but they usually describe the same thing: the overarching goal of an organization.

Not surprisingly, Best-of-the-Best organizations do an especially better job communicating their vision of the future, listing company goals, and ensuring employees are clear on what goals and results they are accountable for achieving.

Statement: "I am clear on my Organization's goals and future direction."

Best-of-the-Best Benchmark:	89.5%
Overall Benchmark:	74.8%
Best-of-the-Best Exceed by:	**+14.7**

Fig. 1: Best-of-the-Best on Vision

Visions do work for the bottom line. Two Stanford professors, James C. Collins and Jerry I. Porras, surveyed CEOs at Fortune 500 and Inc. 100 companies to identify organizations they thought were "visionary" and compared them with their competitors. Going back to 1926, they showed that if you invested one imaginary dollar in a general mutual fund, by 1990 your dollar would have grown to $415. But, if you invested that same imaginary dollar with visionary companies, in 1990 your $1 would have grown to $6,356. Aren't those the types of results you and your organization are seeking? For more details, read *Built to Last: Successful Habits of Visionary Companies* (Collins & Porras, 1994).

However, the problem with "vision" is threefold. First, some organizations do not have a clear vision of where they are heading. As one employee told us, "I love reading mysteries, but I do not enjoy working in the middle of one."

TIP

Would you like to have the specific steps to creating a compelling, positive vision? Go to www.peter stark.com, and enter the word ENGAGE in the Tip Box.

Second, some organizations state a vision, but do not live the vision or bring it to a reality. At one organization, the executives passed out little cards printed with the new vision. That was the last time the employees heard about it. Even worse, the actions of the managers at the company were the antithesis of what was in the vision. Employees are motivated by what they see on a daily basis in the halls, not what they read on the walls.

Statement: "Our daily business practices are consistent with our mission statement."

Best-of-the-Best Benchmark:	90.2%
Overall Benchmark:	79.7%
Best-of-the-Best Exceed by:	**+10.5**

Fig. 2: Best-of-the-Best on Consistent Business Practices

The third problem is not creating an organizational structure that supports the vision and instead focuses on personalities. Although it generates lots of work for consultants, designing organizational charts around "who plays nice together or who doesn't" is not in the organization's best interest. A structure that is most effective at assisting the organization to achieve its vision leads to superior results.

Statement: "My company's organizational structure supports our ability to accomplish our vision and goals."

Best-of-the-Best Benchmark:	75.5%
Overall Benchmark:	62.2%
Best-of-the-Best Exceed by:	**+13.3**

Fig. 3: Best-of-the-Best on Organizational Structure

A vision can be an incredibly powerful tool for managers and supervisors. When Louis Gerstner Jr. took charge of IBM in 1993, the company was in turmoil and the company's annual net losses reached a record $8 billion. At the time Gerstner was quoted as saying, "The last thing IBM needs is a vision." Only a year later, in 1994, he conceded that IBM did require some long-range thinking. An incredible turnaround story began as a result of the vision that emerged from a strategic planning session.

IBM's senior management team articulated the focus of strength for the company and in 1995, Gerstner communicated IBM's new vision: Network computing would drive the next phase of industry growth and would be the company's overarching strategy. This vision and long-range strategy sent IBM on a series of acquisitions that positioned network services to become the fastest growing segment of the company. IBM's extraordinary turnaround demonstrated that the most important thing the organization needed was a shared vision.

A clear vision and strategic goals are forces that encourage and energize people. A great vision is radical, compelling, and heartfelt. Vision comes from the heart and creates passion in both people and organizations. It's a vision because you can see it.

What the Best-of-the-Best organizations do differently than others is ensure that they possess a compelling, positive vision, known by every employee, along with goals and the company's future direction. When people are clear on the destination, are given a map to get to the destination, and a tour guide communicating along the way, they will not only support the expedition, they will really enjoy the trip.

If you want to increase motivation, raise morale, and promote even higher levels of productivity, define a compelling, positive vision.

Key #2: Communication—The Right Stuff at the Right Time

Have you ever felt this way, or worked for someone who seemed to believe that employees don't:

- Need corporate information to do their jobs?
- "Get it" so there's no need to bother passing along pertinent information?
- Care about strategic direction?

Whether these are real reasons or excuses, when managers hold these beliefs and don't communicate to employees, the relationship between managers, employees, and the organization almost always deteriorates. When employees do not feel that their opinions and thoughts are welcomed or valued, they eventually stop making suggestions or decisions and just do what they are told. That's not the attitude that brings success.

Real communication, whether in a personal relationship or an organization, is difficult to get right. People are busy and it is hard to find the time to communicate. But it can be done. The Best-of-the-Best organizations value two-way communication between management and employees instead of only the top-down directive communication that happens in many organizations.

Best-of-the-Best leaders make an effort to seek out the thoughts and opinions of employees. They expect employees to think and make decisions that improve the company. And they are in the habit of seeking the thoughts and opinions of employees prior to making changes that impact their work.

Statement: "Managers and supervisors at my organization seek the opinions and thoughts of the employees who work here."

Best-of-the-Best Benchmark:	79.8%
Overall Benchmark:	61.6%
Best-of-the-Best Exceed by:	**+18.2**

Fig. 4: Best-of-the-Best on Seeking Employee Opinions

An 18.2 percentage point difference is a competitive weapon in the business of employee engagement. If more of your employees are fully engaged, knowing that their thoughts and opinions make a difference to their organization's success, you are likely to have a more productive, profitable organization with higher levels of customer satisfaction compared with your competitors.

You've probably experienced a delay between the time senior management knows about something and the time the front line learns about the information. In some organizations communication happens very quickly; in others, it could take months or even years. Managers who are good communicators believe employees need to know the information to do their jobs.

> You will find that there are very few things in organizations that are truly "confidential."

Of course, once one person in an organization knows the information, eventually their peers are in the loop, and the information trickles down to everyone—even if the information is now inaccurate or embellished. You will find that there are very few things in organizations that are truly "confidential."

Statement: *"When good or bad things happen at my organization, employees hear about it in a timely manner."*

Best-of-the-Best Benchmark:	81.9%
Overall Benchmark:	63.1%
Best-of-the-Best Exceed by:	**+18.8**

Fig. 5: Best-of-the-Best on Sharing Information

The more that sensitive or "un-discussable" topics are kept from employees or lower layers of management, the more employees will feel that management does not trust them. As a result, employees will find it difficult to do their jobs.

As part of an employee survey process, one manager stated he did not share information with his staff because "employees do not see the big picture." However, each of his employees eventually did hear the information and then, one by one, went to the manager to ask if it was accurate.

Most companies have some type of regularly scheduled management team meeting. When the meeting is over, the Best-of-the-Best managers are significantly better at making sure their employees know about the organization's future plans.

Statement: *"My supervisor/manager keeps us informed about our organization's plans."*

Best-of-the-Best Benchmark:	87.2%
Overall Benchmark:	72.5%
Best-of-the-Best Exceed by:	**+14.7**

Fig. 6: Best-of-the-Best on Sharing Company Plans

There are the plans and then there are changes to the plans. To be successful, organizations need to change course and adjust plans. These changes also need to be communicated quickly. Imagine your frustration and embarrassment if you were a manager whose opinion survey reflected this comment: "I am angry. I have been working on this project, which I learned just last week was cancelled 60 days ago."

Statement: "When changes are made at my organization, I hear about it in a timely manner."

Best-of-the-Best Benchmark:	71.1%
Overall Benchmark:	60.1%
Best-of-the-Best Exceed by:	**+11.0**

Fig. 7: Best-of-the-Best on Timely Communication

Senior management plays a significant role in the overall communication that flows down to employees. When the CEO or president regularly communicates with all employees, whether through e-mail, video, or a town hall meeting, most employees appreciate the communication. The challenge for senior managers is that they will never be fully effective at getting the communication down to the front lines unless they are supported by managers and supervisors who place a high value on making sure employees are "in the loop."

Statement: "Communication flows effectively from upper management to employees."

Best-of-the-Best Benchmark:	64.6%
Overall Benchmark:	52.3%
Best of the Best Exceed by:	**+12.3**

Fig. 8: Best-of-the-Best on Communication Flow

Get the lag time out of your organization's communication. The faster senior and middle managers, along with immediate supervisors, can get the communication down to the front lines, the better-equipped employees will be to make the right decisions and provide extraordinary service.

Key #3: Select the Right People for the Right Job

Sit back and think for a minute about how the people you manage feel about their colleagues. Would they say that you hired excellent team members who were an asset to the organization? In the minds of their employees, the Best-of-the-Best organizations are 20 percentage points higher than organizations in the Overall Benchmark.

When your organization acquires a reputation for workplace excellence, you tend to attract a higher caliber candidate to interview. If your organization has a reputation for hiring those people, you are not going to take on a mediocre or poor candidate. Like the Best-of-the-Best organizations, you would rather wait and re-post the job than give the position to a candidate who is not a fit.

Statement: "My organization hires the most qualified candidates possible."

Best-of-the-Best Benchmark:	79.8%
Overall Benchmark:	59.6%
Best-of-the-Best Exceed by:	**+20.2**

Fig. 9: Best-of-the-Best on Hiring Qualified Candidates

In Best-of-the-Best organizations, multiple people interview the candidate. More people give input to determine if the candidate is a fit, both technically and as a team member.

Another feature that separates the Best-of-the-Best organizations is that the hiring process and new employee orientation are a big deal. These organizations know that they spend valuable time and money finding the right person for the job. They want to do everything they possibly can to ensure the employee's, and the organization's, success.

Result: The Best-of-the-Best organizations are significantly better at carefully aligning the employee to the organization.

Statement: "New people are carefully oriented to 'the way we do things around here.'"

Best-of-the-Best Benchmark:	79.7%
Overall Benchmark:	65.5%
Best-of-the-Best Exceed by:	**+14.2**

Fig. 10: Best-of-the-Best on Orientation

Best-of-the-Best organizations are significantly different because they promote qualified, well-trained people into positions of management. If an individual supervisor or manager plays a leadership role in creating workplace excellence, then it makes sense that this leader is promoted into a leadership position.

Statement: "My organization promotes qualified, well-trained employees to management."

Best-of-the-Best Benchmark:	73.8%
Overall Benchmark:	60.9%
Best-of-the-Best Exceed by:	**+12.9**

Fig. 11: Best-of-the-Best on Promotion to Management

Selecting the right leader is critical to your organization's success. Whether an employee leaves your company at the end of the day saying "I love my job" or "I don't get paid enough to put up with this crap" depends on the relationship the employee has with his or her immediate supervisor. Give an employee an excellent leader and you radically increase your chance of being rated as a Best-of-the-Best organization. (Give an employee a great leader who, as you will read in

Key #8, provides the employee with growth opportunities, and you have an even bigger chance of being an employer of choice.)

Key #4: Remember, We're on the Same Team

When it comes to organizational success, individuals cannot win without a team. Teams cannot win without the contributions of individual team members. Michael Jordan, the NBA legend, had it right when he stated that it was important for everyone to remember that "there is no 'I' in team, but there is an 'I' in win." To consistently win, you need both great players and great teamwork.

It is important that each team member take responsibility, be accountable, and produce extraordinary results so the team can win. The Best-of-the-Best organizations understand the fine balance between teamwork and individual contributions.

Statement: "My organization places a high value on teamwork."

Best-of-the-Best Benchmark:	92.0%
Overall Benchmark:	80.7%
Best-of-the-Best Exceed by:	**+11.3**

Fig. 12: Best-of-the-Best on Valuing Teamwork

Over 80% of respondents in both benchmarks say they value teamwork. It is the breadth of teamwork that separates the Best-of-the-Best organizations from the rest.

Statement: "Our department works well as a team."

Best-of-the-Best Benchmark:	89.9%
Overall Benchmark:	78.9%
Best-of-the-Best Exceed by:	**+11.0**

Fig. 13: Best-of-the-Best on Intradepartmental Teamwork

Almost everyone in both benchmarks agrees that teamwork is a strength within their own departments. What is particularly different about the Best-of-the-Best is that they are not only stronger at teamwork in their own departments, but cross-departmentally as well.

Statement: "In my organization, the departments cooperate well together."

Best-of-the-Best Benchmark:	80.3%
Overall Benchmark:	64.3%
Best-of-the-Best Exceed by:	**+16.0**

Fig. 14: Best-of-the-Best on Cross-departmental Teamwork

While all organizations struggle with cross-departmental communication, the Best-of-the-Best organizations are significantly better at it than are organizations in the Overall Benchmark.

Statement: "Information is well-communicated between departments."

Best-of-the-Best Benchmark:	64.9%
Overall Benchmark:	51.6%
Best-of-the-Best Exceed by:	**+13.3**

Fig. 15: Best-of-the-Best on Cross-departmental Communication

Once you build teamwork in your own department, you can rise above the rest by extending that teamwork and communication to other departments.

Teamwork—the actions, not just the talk—begins with you. Your leadership style is essential to executing that vision by communicating the essential information about your strategies and projects up, down, and across the organization.

Key #5: Cool Stuff—Continuous Improvement and Innovation

Many times after working with a Best-of-the-Best client, we return to the office and share with our staff the "cool stuff"—creating new products, processes, or services; or solving significant organizational or industry problems—a client is working on. Anything other than performing the day-to-day components of the job can fall into the category of "cool stuff."

For Betteravia Farms, one of the largest produce farms in California, innovation is a core component of its business practices. Fifteen years ago, Betteravia watered crops by flooding the rows. Fertilizers were applied by driving a tractor through the fields. Through employee ideas and a continual goal of improving efficiency, new systems were developed. Today, all of the crops are watered and fertilized through pinholes in a drip tape buried two inches in the ground. A GPS guided tractor plants the seeds directly over the pinholes. These innovations have saved the farm millions of dollars annually.

What is important to emphasize is that "cool stuff" is all about innovation, continuous improvement, and change. And change makes most people uncomfortable.

An interesting finding from the benchmarks was that the Best-of-the-Best leaders do a better job of keeping their employees "uncomfortable." Some people have told us in strong words that "uncomfortable" is a wrong feeling to stir up within an employee. But uncomfortable is exactly what people feel when they are expected to add value to the organization by working on "cool stuff."

We know that organizations are able to achieve what they value, expect, and recognize. The Best-of-the-Best organizations do an especially better job of establishing an environment where employees are expected and encouraged to improve quality in the organization. This is a very different environment from one where innovation relies on an employee suggestion box that's checked once a month just in case someone ventures to drop in a comment.

Statement: "I am encouraged to take the initiative to improve quality in my area."

Best-of-the-Best Benchmark:	91.4%
Overall Benchmark:	65.8%
Best-of-the-Best Exceed by:	**+25.6**

Fig. 16: Best-of-the-Best on Encouraging Innovation

Encouragement is a good thing. The Best-of-the-Best organizations have learned that setting expectations regarding continuous improvement—like including the topic on annual performance reviews—is even better. Organizations get what they expect and what they measure.

Statement: "People at my organization are expected to come up with new innovative ideas."

Best-of-the-Best Benchmark:	79.5%
Overall Benchmark:	67.6%
Best-of-the-Best Exceed by:	**+11.9**

Fig. 17: Best-of-the-Best on Expecting Innovation

People know they are encouraged to improve quality and come up with innovative ideas when they are recognized for exhibiting those behaviors. Recognizing employees who worked on "cool stuff" sends a message to all employees that innovation and quality are important.

Statement: "People in my organization are recognized when they come up with innovative ideas."

Best-of-the-Best Benchmark:	84.5%
Overall Benchmark:	60.1%
Best-of-the-Best Exceed by:	**+24.4**

Fig. 18: Best-of-the-Best on Recognizing Innovation

Statement: "My organization places a high value on continuous improvement."

Best-of-the-Best Benchmark:	90.9%
Overall Benchmark:	76.9%
Best-of-the-Best Exceed by:	**+14.0**

Fig. 19: Best-of-the-Best on Continuous Improvement

Although we have no scientific proof, we believe the leaders in the Best-of-the-Best organizations sleep better at night because they spend less time lying awake worrying about problems to fix or conflicts to resolve. In the Best-of-the-Best organizations, employees are clear that it is their job to fix the problem and that management will be receptive to their recommendations and recognize their innovative contributions.

Being leaders in innovation, the Best-of-the-Best companies are learning organizations that continuously try to "outlearn" their competition by thinking, testing, and eventually implementing new and better ways to improve the organization. The Best-of-the-Best organizations make innovation and problem solving—and the recognition of the individuals who do these activities—an important part of their culture.

> If your organization emulates the Best-of-the-Best in this category, you may be marketing the next Teflon, Post-it Notes, or even Viagra.

If your organization emulates the Best-of-the-Best in this category, you may be marketing the next Teflon, Post-it Notes, or even Viagra. All of these products were accidental inventions developed by people working for organizations that valued and recognized continuous improvement and innovation.

Key #6: Recognize and Reward Excellent Performance

Does your organization value all employees? Perhaps the answer that goes through your mind is, "Yes, our people are our most important asset." Now ask yourself, does your organization: Reward employees who are mediocre or poor performers? Distribute bonuses solely based on the number of years of service to your organization?

If you want your organization to be included in the Best-of-the-Best Benchmark, you must answer the last two questions with an emphatic "NO."

When every employee receives the same reward, or when rewards are not linked directly to performance and results, it is almost guaranteed to lead to lower morale. The Best-of-the-Best organizations demonstrate that they value the people in their companies who are the most successful at achieving positive results and living the organization's vision and values.

For service organizations, *people* are the only asset.

Statement: "I feel my organization appropriately rewards the highest achievers."

Best-of-the-Best Benchmark:	73.4%
Overall Benchmark:	55.8%
Best-of-the-Best Exceed by:	**+17.6**

Fig. 20: Best-of-the-Best on Performance Rewards

The Best-of-the-Best organizations look for opportunities to tell others about an employee's excellent performance. Will some people be offended that they were not also publicly recognized? Yes, but the Best-of-the-Best organizations feel that the benefit to the organization of acknowledging outstanding individual or team performance is well worth the risk of upsetting someone who was not recognized.

Statement: "When someone performs well in our organization, others are informed of the success."

Best-of-the-Best Benchmark:	80.2%
Overall Benchmark:	65.4%
Best-of-the-Best Exceed by:	**+14.8**

Fig. 21: Best-of-the-Best on Communicating Outstanding Performance

When organizations appropriately reward and publicly recognize high performance, people feel appreciated.

Statement: "I feel appreciated for my contributions to my organization."

Best-of-the-Best Benchmark:	82.3%
Overall Benchmark:	63.3%
Best-of-the-Best Exceed by:	**+19.0**

Statement: "I receive credit and recognition when I do a good job."

Best-of-the-Best Benchmark:	86.7%
Overall Benchmark:	70.6%
Best-of-the-Best Exceed by:	**+16.1**

Fig. 22: Best-of-the-Best on Appreciating Employee Contributions

> **People who truly feel valued want to stay in the relationship.**

Feeling appreciated is intangible and hard to describe. When people do not believe their unique contributions are valued, they tend to feel that they are treated like a commodity. When you are a commodity, it does not matter who does your job, as long as it gets done.

Best-of-the-Best organizations do the necessary things: appropriately reward the highest achievers and then tell the world about positive performance. The result is their employees feel that the unique "gifts" they bring to work each day are valued. People who truly feel valued want to stay in the relationship.

Key #7: Accountability Counts

Performance management is handled very differently in the Best-of-the-Best organizations in three distinct areas. First, the Best-of-the-Best are better at clearly defining what is expected from employees. Second, they excel in the area of giving employees feedback regarding their performance. And third, the Best-of-the-Best are better at holding all members of the team accountable to performance standards.

Employees need to see the target they are trying to hit. The Best-of-the-Best organizations do a much better job at ensuring that job responsibilities are clearly defined for every employee. Employees need and want to be clear on their organizational responsibilities.

Statement: "Job responsibilities at my organization are clearly defined."

Best-of-the-Best Benchmark:	85.1%
Overall Benchmark:	71.7%
Best-of-the-Best Exceed by:	**+13.4**

Fig. 23: Best-of-the-Best on Clearly Defined Job Responsibilities

A related area where the Best-of-the-Best lead is in ensuring that employees know how performance will be measured. Many employees have a double whammy going against them. They are not clear on their job responsibilities, and the performance standards are unclear. This is the equivalent of blindfolding the employees and then directing them to spend their time playing the organizational version of "pin the tail on the donkey." When you are blindfolded, it is just about impossible to hit the goal.

Statement: "I have a good understanding of the performance standards/measurements at my organization."

Best-of-the-Best Benchmark:	92.5%
Overall Benchmark:	82.7%
Best-of-the-Best Exceed by:	**+9.8**

Fig. 24: Best-of-the-Best on Performance Standards

Providing performance feedback to employees is the second area in this key where the Best-of-the-Best organizations excel. To be useful, feedback must help people learn, grow, and improve. Best-of-the-Best companies are better than average at determining performance measures and coaching staff on how to reach or exceed them.

Statement: "My performance review provides me with feedback that helps me learn, grow, and improve my performance."

Best-of-the-Best Benchmark:	80.7%
Overall Benchmark:	69.2%
Best-of-the-Best Exceed by:	**+11.5**

Fig. 25: Best-of-the-Best on Performance Reviews

When an employee's review is completed on time, and it is thorough, accurate, and provides examples for growth and development, it tells the employee that the supervisor cares about the employee.

Another piece the Best-of-the-Best contribute to completing the performance management and accountability puzzle is in the area of ongoing feedback. "Timely" ongoing feedback doesn't rely solely on a performance review, which may be conducted once, or perhaps twice, a year. If you only communicate once a year, how can you foster teamwork, solve problems, encourage innovation, and reward performance? Immediate, ongoing feedback keeps you in contact with your staff and opens the door to them. When there is a performance issue, you deal with it immediately.

Statement: "My supervisor gives me good ongoing feedback regarding my performance."

Best-of-the-Best Benchmark:	82.7%
Overall Benchmark:	73.0%
Best-of-the-Best Exceed by:	**+9.7**

Fig. 26: Best-of-the-Best on Timely Ongoing Feedback

Although some argue it may be difficult for employees to determine accountability throughout the organization, one area where most employees see a very clear picture of reality is with the level of accountability that exists in their own departments. By watching the daily behavior of the individuals on their team, employees know if other team members are held accountable to meet team goals.

To rise to the level of the Best-of-the-Best organizations, you need to be good at three things:

■ Clearly defining job responsibilities and ensuring employees understand those job responsibilities

- Providing ongoing, timely feedback that helps employees learn and grow
- Holding people accountable to meeting those responsibilities

Key #8: Every Employee Learns and Grows

A manager once said to us, "I don't like some of the questions on your survey because my employees do not want to grow. They want to come to work each day, put their heads down, and do their jobs." This was the same manager who told us he did not want to provide training for his employees because they would just quit and take their new skills to another employer.

If you can relate to this manager's concern, there is a strong possibility your department scores would not match the Best-of-the-Best Benchmark. The problem with maintaining a bunch of untrained employees in your department who do not want to learn and grow is that they are going to be working for you the rest of their careers. These employees have few options and no Best-of-the-Best organization will want to hire them.

Statement: "My organization places a high value on training and educating employees."

Best-of-the-Best Benchmark:	81.2%
Overall Benchmark:	69.4%
Best-of-the-Best Exceed by:	**+11.8**

Fig. 27: Best-of-the-Best on Training and Education

Why would employees want to be with your organization three years from now? There is a good chance they hope your organization is going to provide them with opportunity for future advancement and training so they can learn and grow.

Statement: "I feel there is sufficient opportunity for advancement at my organization."

Best-of-the-Best Benchmark:	78.7%
Overall Benchmark:	66.5%
Best-of-the-Best Exceed by:	**+12.2**

Fig. 28: Best-of-the-Best on Opportunity for Advancement

Best-of-the-Best organizations succeed at creating an environment where employees want to work for them in the future by providing useful training and learning opportunities. The training may be provided inside your own department and it may be provided formally by the organizational development professionals in your company.

Statement: "I feel my organization has a good training program."

Best-of-the-Best Benchmark:	84.1%
Overall Benchmark:	69.4%
Best-of-the-Best Exceed by:	**+14.7**

Fig. 29: Best-of-the-Best on Quality Training

Employees who work in the Best-of-the-Best organizations get access to good training programs. This is a positive reflection on the work of all the trainers and human resource professionals who struggle for proof that training makes a difference. But organizational development professionals cannot rest on their laurels just because there is a good program. The training has to be relevant to both the employee's and the organization's success.

Statement: "The training I receive is useful and helps me to do a better job."

Best-of-the-Best Benchmark:	86.3%
Overall Benchmark:	73.8%
Best-of-the-Best Exceed by:	**+12.5**

Fig. 30: Best-of-the-Best on Training Effectiveness

People who feel well trained to do the job they currently do and are confident that the organization will provide them with future opportunity, will most likely want to stay with their current organization. So we must ask: As a manager, are you encouraging staff to take advantage of these opportunities?

When you do a better job selecting the right people, and then do a better job training those people, you are going to give your organization a significant competitive advantage in your industry.

Key #9: Problems ... No Problem

While 73% of the employees in the Overall Benchmark believe their organizations want them to solve problems, only 60% say they are recognized for innovative ideas, which is a 13.1 percentage point difference. The organizations in the Best-of-the-Best Benchmark do a particularly better job at both recognizing employees and ensuring them that management wants them to solve problems.

Statement: "Employees at my organization believe management wants them to solve problems."

Best-of-the-Best Benchmark:	90.1%
Overall Benchmark:	73.3%
Best-of-the-Best Exceed by:	**+16.8**

Fig. 31: Best-of-the-Best on Problem Solving

The Best-of-the-Best are also better than organizations in the Overall Benchmark in quickly resolving conflict in their organizations. Conflict causes people to be sidetracked by peripheral issues rather than staying focused on achieving the mission, vision, and goals of the organization.

Statement: "When conflict arises in my organization, it is resolved in a timely manner."

Best-of-the-Best Benchmark:	77.4%
Overall Benchmark:	64.3%
Best-of-the-Best Exceed by:	**+13.3**

Fig. 32: Best-of-the-Best on Timely Conflict Resolution

One could make a case that the problems employees encounter may not be performance related. The challenge with this is that people make, and fix, problems. When problems are not fixed in a timely manner, they are allowed to linger. It has been our experience that most people are able to identify problems quickly. What makes the Best-of-the-Best organizations so different is that they not only identify the problem fast, they do a considerably better job resolving the problem.

Statement: "At my organization, problems are identified and handled in the early stages."

Best-of-the-Best Benchmark:	75.8%
Overall Benchmark:	60.3%
Best-of-the-Best Exceed by:	**+15.5**

Fig. 33: Best-of-the-Best on Problem Identification

Key #10: It's All About the Customer

One thing that is easy to agree on is that terrific customer service is really hard to find.

In the extended studies program at San Diego State University, we've given hundreds of students the following assignment: Over the next two weeks, become a mystery shopper at ten businesses you frequent. Rate the level of service you are provided as: Great, Good, Fair, or Poor. The results are always the same. The average percentage of businesses with a service level rated as "Great" is approximately 20%.

> One thing that is easy to agree on is that terrific customer service is really hard to find.

Almost all employees say their organizations place a high value on customer service. What is important is that 94% of the people working for the Best-of-the-Best say their organizations place a high value on *exceeding* customer expectations.

Statement: "My organization places a high value on exceeding customer expectations."

Best-of-the-Best Benchmark:	93.7%
Overall Benchmark:	83.3%
Best-of-the-Best Exceed by:	**+10.4**

Fig. 34: Best-of-the-Best on Valuing Customer Service

Although employees in both benchmarks say their organizations place a high value on customer service, the Best-of-the-Best are notably better at providing the managerial support employees require to accomplish that goal.

Statement: "People at my organization are free to communicate up the ladder to get answers to customer requests."

Best-of-the-Best Benchmark:	86.9%
Overall Benchmark:	72.9%
Best-of-the-Best Exceed by:	**+14.0**

Fig. 35: Best-of-the-Best on Taking Initiative in Customer Service

The Best-of-the-Best understand that everyone in the organization either directly serves the customer or directly supports someone who serves the customer. With management's strong willingness to serve employees, it is easier to create an environment in which customers love to do business with an organization.

Have you ever received poor customer service because of a stupid policy, procedure, or system? If you are a resident of San Diego who wants to reserve a city park for a Boy Scout or Girl Scout event, you have to drive to downtown San Diego through a lot of traffic and with few options for parking to hand in an application in person. You cannot do it by mail, Federal Express, or e-mail. But, if you live outside of San Diego County you can simply mail in the application. Why the difference? The employees at the city parks department don't know. They only know the rule. (Steele, SignOnSanDiego.com, February 17, 2007)

This is an excellent example of designing a policy, procedure, and system that ensures customers will complain. This type of policy most likely would not be adopted by an organization in the Best-of-the-Best Benchmark.

Statement: "My organization's policies, procedures, and systems support me in providing quality customer service."

Best-of-the-Best Benchmark:	89.0%
Overall Benchmark:	75.3%
Best-of-the-Best Exceed by:	**+13.7**

Fig. 36: Best-of-the-Best on Customer Service Systems

The Best-of-the-Best organizations understand that to have customers experience your company, thank you for the great service, and become loyal advocates who are five times more likely to refer your business to other customers, you need the right policies, procedures, systems, and environment in place.

You'll also see that Best-of-the-Best organizations are significantly better at ensuring their employees have the right support to get the job done.

Statement: "I have the tools and equipment I need to do a good job."

Best-of-the-Best Benchmark:	90.2%
Overall Benchmark:	78.0%
Best-of-the-Best Exceed by:	**+12.2**

Fig. 37: Best-of-the-Best on Tools That Support Customer Service

Last, the Best-of-the-Best organizations are better at building a working environment that supports employees in exceeding customer expectations.

Statement: "The working environment in my area supports us in providing top-quality customer service."

Best-of-the-Best Benchmark:	90.2%
Overall Benchmark:	80.0%
Best-of-the-Best Exceed by:	**+10.2**

Fig. 38: Best-of-the-Best on Creating an Environment Conducive to Customer Service

It is not a surprise that over 80% of employees in the Overall Benchmark agreed that their organizations place a high value on customer service. Compared to the average competitor in the market-place, companies that care enough to conduct an employee opinion survey are probably really good at providing service to their customers. Besides, it is hard to stay in business long without a monopoly if your customers are continuously not satisfied.

It is the additional ten-percentage point difference in providing the *support* for that service that gives the Best-of-the-Best companies an appreciably competitive advantage. Supporting their employees allows them to provide customers with the quality service they desire.

A foundation of strong communication and support ensures that the right policies, procedures, systems, tools, and equipment are in place. The resulting environment allows employees to provide a level of exceptional service.

Why wouldn't customers love to do business with the Best-of-the-Best organizations?

SOMETHING IS MISSING—SHOW ME THE MONEY!

When we talk about these ten keys with clients, invariably someone asks, "Where's the money? Isn't wage or salary one of the key differentiators between the Best-of-the-Best organizations and the rest of the pack?" The answer is a little bit of yes and a lot of no.

There is only a 5.9 percentage point difference between Best-of-the-Best companies (67.9%) and Overall Benchmark companies (62.0%) when employees responded to the statement, "Compared to a similar position in my industry and geographic location, I am fairly compensated."

A variance of six percentage points is not significant, particularly when you look at the employees' responses to statements reported in "The 10 Keys to Workplace Excellence" section.

Did you expect a bigger monetary difference between the Best-of-the-Best organizations and the Overall Benchmarks? Not only is there not much difference, but during the last three years the gap between the two has continued to shrink. The reason is simple. To hire and retain an employee, both the overall organizations and the Best-of-the-Best organizations need to pay a competitive wage. Most employees would not join a new company to take home a lower wage than they currently earn. All companies must be competitive unless they are seeking unemployed candidates who are willing to take any job at any wage.

Whenever an employee leaves a company, most often the manager will say, "The employee left for a ton of money and there is no way we could counter the amount and get the employee to stay." As stated in the previous chapter, the average amount of wage increase employees receive upon leaving your organization is only approximately 6%. And the reason they leave is because they do not love their jobs or feel a strong relationship with their bosses. When they love their jobs and have a strong effective working relationship with their managers, it takes significantly more than 6% to get people to jump ship.

> **TIP**
>
> Want to learn more ways to motivate your team without money? Go to www.peterstark.com, and enter the word ENGAGE in the Tip Box.

Money is used as the excuse to leave for two reasons. First, employees are not real excited about telling the people who will be providing them with an employment reference that they were a bad or mediocre manager. Second, if managers can blame the exit on money, they do not have to accept any responsibility for the employee leaving. Hence, there is nothing the manager can do about losing good people until someone in power fixes the salaries.

BEGIN TO MAKE A DIFFERENCE

You can do what the best organizations do. Use The 10 Keys to Workplace Excellence. Start with a compelling, positive vision that can be reached by defining clear and concrete goals. Add in an ongoing attitude that more communication to employees is better, and hire and train the people who are receptive to communication and achieving the company vision. Foster teamwork, both within your own department and with other departments.

Move forward with large quantities of encouragement to improve the product, service, and the organization. Hold people accountable and continually recognize excellent performance. Offer the training and opportunities people need to perform well, and make sure they have the resources to provide customer service that generates customer satisfaction.

The most important aspect to remember is that it's up to the individual to utilize his or her leadership skills to use the keys.

PART TWO

If You're a Manager Who Wants to Be a Leader, You Need Followers

Being the Leader Who Makes a Difference

It's easy to get fired up about the most recent managerial "buzz." We've lived through Quality Circles, TQM, Management by Walking Around, shifting paradigms, scorecards, dashboards, Hedgehogs, Black Belt, Lean Manufacturing, the right habits, different hats, and many others.

All those management principles offer something useful. Still, it's not necessary to jump on the newest trend to be a great leader. In our years of interacting with hundreds of organizations and thousands of managers, we have seen a similarity between the things managers do that get them into trouble and the things leaders do that earn faithful followers.

Those insights, based on the benchmark results and what we've learned in our work with leaders in organizations, are profound yet relatively easy to understand. More importantly, they flow from what we've learned from working with employees in these same organizations.

As you read through this list, you may be tempted to say, "This isn't rocket science." We would agree with you. But, if it's so simple and straightforward, why don't more managers practice The 10 Keys to Workplace Excellence to improve their leadership ability and develop a great working environment?

EXCUSES STINK

While reviewing the results of an employee opinion survey, many CEOs or senior management team members have asked, "When so many people who work here are really happy, how can employees in three low-rated departments be so unhappy? When you look at the data, it looks like people are working for a totally different organization. How can this be?"

The answer is this: The difference in how employees feel about the organization is in direct correlation to the quality of their leaders.

Culture in organizations is not easy to change. Both managers and employees become accustomed to the organization's environment and can take a "that's the way we are here" attitude. Some of the low-performing managers we have interviewed shared reasons for their low scores. The reasons include:

- That is the way the board, CEO, or senior management team is and things will never change.
- We do not pay people enough, and I get no support from HR or senior management to give them a raise.
- HR will not support managers, so performance problems will never be addressed.
- Too many people in the organization are protected like sacred cows.
- People in the organization don't understand what our department is "all about."
- The industry, or this position, has high turnover.
- The employees don't have a firm grasp on reality.
- The employees will never be happy.

- The low scores are a reflection of another manager or supervisor, not me.
- I will never create an organization that is "touchy-feely."
- The employees did not understand the questions when taking the survey.

Whether managers believe they can positively influence the work environment for the employees in their areas, or believe they cannot, it is important to note: THEY ARE RIGHT!

If managers believe they can create workplace excellence, they likely utilize the seventy-six strategies you'll learn about in chapter six. If managers believe there is not much they can do, they tend not to take action, confirming their negative beliefs. Our research solidly confirms this, regardless of what anyone in the organization thinks.

> **Whether managers believe they can positively influence the work environment for the employees in their areas, or believe they cannot, it is important to note: THEY ARE RIGHT!**

One manager can make the difference. If you want to change the work environment, change the way you manage.

DEVELOP A POSITIVE, COMPELLING VISION OF THE FUTURE

We challenge each leader to consider his or her personal, individual vision and how it impacts the organization.

"Vision" is not another fad. It is the first step here, and the first of The 10 Keys to Workplace Excellence, for a reason. A compelling vision and clearly articulated goals are the foundation of Best-of-the-Best organizations. Every leader has a type of a vision. Which of the following matches your outlook?

The first vision type is positive and uplifting: "Today is a great day and tomorrow is going to be even better." Leaders with positive visions take the necessary actions to make the department even more productive and the environment an even better place to do the work.

The second vision type is what we call status quo: "Today is okay and I'm hoping that tomorrow will be all right, too." These managers are trying to hang on to their current situation. The ultimate goal of a manager with a status quo vision is to keep things from getting worse.

The third vision type is negative: "If you think today is bad, just wait until tomorrow. It's going to get worse!" These managers usually choose to take no action—and things do get worse.

Only a positive vision can inspire. Leaders with a clear idea of what they stand for and where they are heading, and have communicated their expectations to employees, are both inspiring *and* easy to follow. Their employees maintain an understanding of the leader's values and can predict how the leader will react in a given situation. It is impossible to keep levels of morale and productivity high if the leader is not a role model for a "can do" positive attitude.

One of the greatest visionaries in history was a man whose first seven businesses failed. Twice bankrupt, on two occasions he spent time in a mental institution. Fired by a newspaper editor for a lack of creativity, he had trouble finding financing to begin constructing his most famous idea. His name was Walt Disney. In 1955, he opened Disneyland in Anaheim, California, even though there were many critics who felt the park would fail.

Nine years later, he began to buy rights to land in Orlando, Florida, to build a second theme park. Unfortunately, Walt Disney did not live long enough to see Orlando's Disney World become a reality. On a behind-the-scenes tour at Disney World, I (Peter) asked the tour guide, a young college student, "Wouldn't it have been great if Walt Disney could have seen Disney World when construction was complete?" The young student replied, "Sir, here at Disney World, we really do believe that Walt did see the completion."

How true. Walt Disney saw the completion before anyone did, and spent his entire life trying to share the vision with others. You can do the same by involving others in creating, clarifying, and crystallizing your organization's vision.

CLARIFY GREAT PERFORMANCE FOR EVERY EMPLOYEE

There is nothing motivating about accomplishing a mediocre goal. When you isolate the leaders of the highest-rated departments and compare them with those in the lowest-rated departments, the most significant difference is in the area of managing an employee's performance.

When employees were asked if their manager set and communicated performance objectives for each employee, the highest-rated leaders achieved a result that was thirty-two percentage points more favorable than the lowest-rated managers.

RECOGNIZE BOTH GREAT AND POOR PERFORMANCE

The next significant difference between managers in the high- and low-performing departments is recognition. When employees responded to this statement, "My manager provides me with adequate recognition for positive performance," the highest-rated departments once again achieved results that were approximately twenty-eight percentage points more favorable than the lowest-rated departments. Great leaders ensure that when an employee does a good job, he or she is recognized.

By interviewing managers who lead the highest- and lowest-rated departments, we have learned that the managers of the highest-rated departments do things differently.

First, they provide recognition immediately after they learn about an employee's positive performance. The longer you wait to do this, the less meaning the recognition will have. If you wait too long, the recognition will actually become a de-motivator for some employees.

Second, the highest-rated managers tend to tailor their recognition to best meet the needs of the employee. For some employees, recognition is most effectively provided one-to-one. For others, recognition may be an e-mail sent to the team or a note written in a newsletter. And for still others, it may be recognition presented in a team meeting.

Third, highly rated leaders encourage other managers and employees on their teams to recognize colleagues who do a great job. This way, recognition becomes part of the team's culture and is not dependent solely on the manager.

> Leaders in the highest-rated departments do not manage performance problems with hope, hint, or prayer.

An observation by Barbara Walters is worth remembering: "To feel valued, to know, even if only once in a while, that you can do a job well is an absolutely marvelous feeling."

Performance problems are also recognized, but differently. Just as managers in the highest-rated departments recognize great performance, they are also notably better when it comes to recognizing performance that is not on target. When employees were asked to rate this statement, "My manager identifies and handles performance problems in the early stages," the managers in the highest-rated departments received a response that was approximately forty percentage points more favorable than the lowest-rated managers.

Leaders in the highest-rated departments do not manage performance problems with hope, hint, or prayer. These high-performing managers get involved with the poor performers to produce a meaningful outcome: either the poor-performing employee corrects the problem or leaves the organization. This action, in the minds of other employees in the department, is crucial.

The managers in the highest-rated departments were approximately twenty-four percentage points better at providing ongoing feedback regarding an employee's performance. What excuses do low-rated managers provide? They are too busy putting out fires set by customers and employees and just "don't have the time" to recognize great performance and quickly address performance problems.

Effective leaders know that providing recognition for meeting and exceeding high performance goals and effectively fixing performance problems is an important part of their jobs.

OVERCOMMUNICATE BECAUSE YOU REALLY CARE

As you saw in The 10 Keys to Workplace Excellence, communication is important if you want to be in the Best-of-the-Best Benchmark. But, once again, when we compare managers in the highest-rated departments with managers in the lowest-rated departments, there are noticeable differences.

The managers in the highest-rated departments figure out how to get information regarding the organization to their employees. When comparing the highest-rated managers with the lowest-rated managers there is an impressive 30 percentage point difference. They specifically relay how the organization's plans will impact the employees, their jobs, and the department. Managers leading high-rated departments know that going out of their way to communicate with employees indirectly tells the employees that they really care about them.

In today's technological world, it is not hard to be accessible or connected to your employees. But, for some reason, the managers in the lowest-rated departments struggle with accessibility. On the survey, employees were asked to respond to this statement: "My manager is easily accessible when needed (for example, in person or by phone, e-mail, and voice mail)." The highest-rated department leaders earned a response that was more favorable by twenty-six percentage points.

The benchmark tells us that when a manager listens to an employee's opinion and acts on the input, the employee feels valued. In fact, managers in the highest-rated departments were rated approximately twenty-three points more favorably by employees in response to "My manager solicits my opinion regarding work affecting my areas of responsibility." The managers in the highest-rated departments understand the importance of involving employees and asking for their opinions on anything that is related to their jobs.

ADMIT IT! YOU MADE A MISTAKE

Sure, this sounds easy enough to do. However, in our experience, only about half of the managerial population is comfortable admitting an error. The other half makes excuses, usually claiming that something outside of their control explains their actions.

Only leaders who feel confident in their ability to lead also feel comfortable admitting when they make a mistake. The benchmarks confirm our experience as executive coaches. When employees were asked to rate the statement, "My manager is able to admit when he makes a mistake," the managers of the highest-rated departments demonstrated a favorable response that was twenty-six percentage points higher than the lowest-rated managers.

Just say, "I messed up. I am sorry. And I am grateful I have the team I do so we can get this problem corrected." Most times, when you can say "I made a mistake," people will go out of their way to forgive you and correct the situation.

OUTWORK EVERYONE ELSE

We are not referring to the number of hours that you put into your job. What we mean is the amount of value you bring to your team or organization. "Outworking" others means you add value by: bringing a compelling positive vision, solving quality or service problems that no one else has solved, dealing with difficult employees or customers, and/or creating an environment where employees love coming to work.

The benchmark data reveal another point. The managers of the highest-rated departments exhibit stronger work habits, which their employees recognize. Managers of the highest-rated departments had a more favorable—by thirty-two percentage points—response to the statement, "My manager sets a good example with his/her work habits."

If your employees do not feel you set a good example with your work habits, lower morale will become prevalent and it will become difficult to ask for, and manage, excellent performance.

TRUST YOUR EMPLOYEES

People do not follow those they do not trust. Trust builds a relationship where employees feel confident about following your lead. When the goals are clear, top-performing managers trust that their employees will get the job done. In response to the benchmark statement, "I trust my manager," the top-performing managers were rated thirty percentage points more favorably than managers of the lowest-rated departments. Managers whose departments rated them so significantly higher know the importance of strong trust.

> **People do not follow those they do not trust.**

The Best-of-the-Best organizations can teach us six important lessons about building trust between the management team and employees.

Trust-Building #1: Clarify, crystallize, and communicate your organization's core values. What do the leaders in your organization say they value? Leaders we work with cite values such as ethical decision making; open, honest, clear, and direct communication; teamwork; results; top-performing employees; satisfied customers; innovation; and work-life balance. What is important is that the leaders can clearly articulate to every employee the values that drive decisions and day-to-day business practices in their organization.

Trust-Building #2: Be consistent. If leaders are clear on the vision and core values, it becomes easier to make consistent decisions. In these companies, an extremely high value is placed on ethical decision making, results, and customer satisfaction.

After a recent keynote speech on employee engagement and workplace excellence, a CEO came up to me (Jane) and said, "I have a vice president that needs to leave our organization. I would like to hire you as a coach so that when I let him go, the VP will know that I did everything possible to try to make the relationship work." For me, it was an easy decision to say, "I don't think that I would make a good coaching fit for your organization." The honest, ethical, and caring thing for this CEO to do in this situation would be to call in the VP and let him go. We value satisfied customers, but we value ethical business practices even more.

In another situation, one of our clients fired a high-performing manager who refused to treat her employees with dignity and respect. When we asked the CEO about making this difficult decision, she replied, "Because of our strong values, this decision was really easy. The only thing that was difficult was the actual meeting where I let the manager go."

Trust-Building #3: Keep your word. Trust is built by doing what you say you are going to do, when you say you are going to do it, even if you no longer feel like doing it. A big challenge for managers is that employee trust recalibrates itself daily in response to leadership decisions and behaviors.

The Best-of-the-Best organizations are appreciably better at doing what they say they are going to do, when they say they are going to do it. In regard to following through and keeping commitments, the Best-of-the-Best Benchmark exceeded the Overall Benchmark by 16.2 percentage points.

Trust-Building #4: Ensure communication is open and honest. Communication from managers regarding the vision, values, and strategic goals is essential to building trust. Honest and direct communication regarding performance also builds trusting relationships. When employees were asked if their company was open and honest with employees, the Best-of-the-Best Benchmark exceeded the Overall Benchmark by 15.1 percentage points.

Trust-Building #5: Involve employees in decisions that impact their work. This seems like common sense since the people who best know how to improve their work are the people doing that work. But, from time to time, we work with managers who say, "These people are so out of touch with reality they do not even know what changes need to take place to make our organization even more successful."

If your goal is to work with an engaged, motivated workforce, you will benefit by involving employees in the decisions that impact their work. If the employees are truly not qualified to do the work, then coach, counsel, and train. And if all that does not work, share them with a competitor.

Trust-Building Lesson #6: Trust employees. The fastest way for a leader to build trust with an employee is to place trust *in* the employee. So go ahead and empower employees to make decisions and increase their responsibilities. Most employees, when given the power to make a decision or take on additional responsibility, will go out of their way not to undermine or erode the trust the leader has placed in them. When employees know they are trusted, they find it much easier to trust management.

Respect and trust have a lot in common. You probably have heard a manager say, "You will have to trust me on this." There is a problem with this line. You can't demand or buy either trust or respect. The managers of the highest-rated departments know that when you give employees a clear goal and then provide frequent, positive, ongoing two-way communication, employees tend to feel respected.

When employees said, "My manager respects me," the managers of the highest-rated departments earned a favorable response that was twenty-two percentage points higher compared to the managers of the lowest-rated departments. And, the managers who lead the highest-rated departments know that it is hard to be a great leader who gives respect without being respected.

THE OUTCOMES ARE PRICELESS

After reviewing the comparisons between the approaches of the highest-rated and the lowest-rated managers, you can see why some employees were so happy and others were not. The outcomes of an environment of workplace excellence are priceless. Employees in the highest-rated departments have a better relationship with their managers, a higher level of trust, and realize that they are respected.

Since you spend approximately 95,000 hours of your life at work, it makes sense that it is easier to love your job when you enjoy a quality working relationship with your boss. When employees responded to, "I have a good working relationship with my manager," the highly rated department managers were forty-three percentage points higher than the lowest-rated managers.

LEADERSHIP MAKES THE DIFFERENCE

Can it be that simple? Yes. Great leaders know employees have choices about where they work. By using what you've learned in this chapter, you can create an environment where people love to come to work and customers love to do business. It may not be rocket science, but it sure works.

This chart shows the percentage point difference between the highest-rated managers and the lowest-rated managers. You can see how one leader can make a difference and how individual leaders can affect the ratings of the entire company

BEST-OF-THE-BEST ON LEADERSHIP	
+40	My manager identifies and handles performance problems in the early stages.
+35	I have a good working relationship with my manager.
+32	My manager sets a good example with his/her work habits.
+32	My manager sets and communicates performance objectives for each associate.
+30	My manager keeps us informed about company plans.
+30	I trust my manager.
+28	My manager provides me with adequate recognition for positive performance.
+26	My manager is easily accessible when needed (for example, in person or by phone, e-mail, and voice mail).
+26	My manager is able to admit when he/she makes a mistake.
+24	My manager gives me good ongoing feedback regarding my performance.
+23	My manager solicits my opinion regarding work affecting my areas of responsibility.
+22	My manager respects me.

The pop quiz on the following page will help you see the leadership areas in which you excel, and the areas where you may need some improvement as you strive to create a workplace where employees love to come to work and customers love to do business.

CREATING WORKPLACE EXCELLENCE—A LEADER'S POP QUIZ

Yes	No	As the leader, I have a positive, compelling vision.
Yes	No	Our team has goals to turn the vision into a reality.
Yes	No	Our goals are a challenge to achieve.
Yes	No	Our team has a plan to turn the goals and vision into reality.
Yes	No	Each member on our team is clear on the goals for his or her position/job.
Yes	No	Team members would say I consistently communicate the company's plans.
Yes	No	Team members would say I consistently communicate the information they need to do their jobs.
Yes	No	Team members would say I want them to solve problems.
Yes	No	Team members would say I promote innovation and improving products, procedures, systems, or services.
Yes	No	Each member of the team makes a contribution to the team's success.
Yes	No	Our team works well together.
Yes	No	Our team works well with other departments/teams in the organization.
Yes	No	On our team, performance problems are resolved in a timely manner.
Yes	No	Our team meets (weekly, bi-weekly) on a regular basis.
Yes	No	We communicate results and our progress toward our goals on a consistent, regular schedule.
Yes	No	Our team produces and achieves outstanding results.
Yes	No	Our team consistently recognizes team and individual success.
Yes	No	Our team knows how to celebrate success.

If you answered yes to more than fifteen questions: You excel as a Best-of-the-Best leader. Congratulations.

If you answered yes to ten to fifteen questions: You are a great leader on the way to becoming even greater. Keep it up.

If you answered yes to less than ten questions: You are on your way to becoming a good leader. Keep reading!

Eleven Stupid Things Managers Do to Mess Up Workplace Excellence

During an interview Pam Smith, deputy director of Health and Human Services for San Diego County, summed up the importance of the manager/employee relationship when she stated, "Great employees deserve great leadership."

Companies do not put The 10 Keys to Workplace Excellence into action—individual managers do.

The enormous amount of data we have collected—analyzing employee opinion survey data by divisions and departments—backs this up. One manager in the organization can wield tremendous influence over how employees feel about their work experience. It doesn't matter if there are 5, 50, 500, or 5,000 employees—if the manager exerts positive leadership, employees will feel positive about their work experience. The same is true if the manager is negative or apathetic about the work experience.

A company may achieve an overall employee opinion survey score that is 81% favorable. In that same company, one department's score may be 92% and another department's or division's score may be 44%. How can this be? Isn't it the same organization with the same vision, values, goals, and strategic initiatives?

> Companies do not put The 10 Keys to Workplace Excellence into action—individual managers do.

The massive swings in employee opinions occur because different managers form different environments inside the same organization. A major contributor to employees' satisfaction, estimated in some surveys to be as much as 70%, is the relationship they experience with their immediate supervisor or manager.

While we could cite extensive research, let it suffice to simply say that organizations attracting, retaining, and motivating the best employees do so by paying a fair market wage and forming an environment where employees love to come to work. Obviously the money is a necessity, but the money alone will not guarantee that people will contribute with their fullest potential. Great organizations know that it is the right relationships at work that attract the best employees and keeps them performing at peak effectiveness.

GREAT EMPLOYEES DESERVE GREAT MANAGERS

We believe that when employees leave your organization, there is a strong possibility they are leaving because of poor leadership. Any manager who has worked in human resources (HR) for longer than a year has heard similar stories over and over again in exit interviews. Based on these exit interviews, HR professionals acquire a pretty strong gut-level feeling for which managers in the organization build relationships where people willingly follow, and which managers in the organization are responsible for employees who are more than willing to share their talents with competitors.

It is important to note that not all employees who leave an organization are examples of "bad" turnover. We strongly believe in the concept of "good" turnover. There are poor-performing employees who are not happy with anyone or anything associated with the organization. Or, these employees do their jobs, but stir up an environment where everyone else suffers. They brighten up the whole company when they depart.

"Bad" turnover occurs when employees who are outstanding contributors to the company's success willingly leave the organization for equal or even less opportunity with another organization—just to escape their boss or intolerable working conditions. When great employees leave it is hard to replace the talent. It also costs a ton of money to train the new employee to be a worthwhile contributor. In many of these situations (although it is hard to admit when it is your department or company), the best employees leave because of poor leadership.

Yet one leader makes a difference. In chapter three, we shared the actions that separate the highest- from the lowest-ranked leaders on employee opinion surveys. While these steps are simple, many managers experience difficulty following them on a consistent basis.

After years of working with organizations and coaching managers, we have identified the eleven stupid things managers do to mess up their organizations, departments, and teams. Most managers could pick out one, or even a few, of the stupid behaviors and say, "Wow, I have done that before." The difference between most managers and the managers who disengage employees and destroy workplace excellence comes down to one word: **FREQUENCY.**

Although all managers who are honest admit they have occasionally slipped and done something stupid in their careers, managers who incite havoc in the workplace put at least one of these stupid things into play with a high level of frequency. Worse yet, many of these managers know they are causing conflict but, for whatever reason, they don't stop doing it. In some cases, once their negative behavior is pointed out to them, they even escalate instances of their poor performance—just because they can.

Stupid Behavior #1: Inability to Control Emotions

When utilized appropriately, emotions are a wonderful human attribute. When used improperly by managers, emotions can devastate organizations and their employees. So number one on our list of stupid behaviors is the inability to control emotions. The worst offenders are managers labeled as "moody."

Recently, in hopes of giving a manager feedback that would enable her to be even more effective, we conducted interviews with fifteen of her employees and peers. All respondents stated that the person's primary opportunity for improvement was to display emotions that were consistent and appropriate to the situation. Examples respondents shared regarding inappropriate leadership behaviors included: raising her voice when she was angry, whether in meetings or in one-on-one communications; sending e-mails that were accusatory in content; and using foul language when she was mad.

Respondents stated you were either on her "good" list, or you were "off" her list, and she ignored you. One employee shared that one time she missed a deadline on a report. When she apologized to this manager for the deadline slipping through the cracks, the manager replied in anger, "Sorry is not good enough. I will never accept an apology for your incompetence."

Finally, if this wasn't enough negative feedback to win someone the label of "moody," respondents went on to add that when this manager came into work each morning, she did not greet or speak to anyone. It was well known around the office that she was not a "morning" person.

During the interview process we were really grateful to one respondent who said, "I hope that you are not planning to give her this feedback until late in the afternoon. She is never good about accepting feedback. But in the morning she is downright nasty!"

When you interview managers who have reputations for being moody or angry, they almost all describe their inappropriate behaviors as "honest or passionate communication." As one manager recently told us, "I am a really honest person. I tell people what I think, right at the moment I think it, and some people cannot handle honest communication." This excuse allows the manager to absolve herself of any responsibility for her employee not accepting how she communicates—the problem is with the employee, not the manager.

The reality of the impact of this type of stupid behavior is that words, once spoken or written, are permanent. The challenge in the above example is that this manager's communication was perceived as angry, inappropriate, and mean-spirited. Yet, if you asked this manager if her goal was to hurt people or undermine employees' levels of commitment and motivation to do a great job, the manager would respond with a resounding, "No, of course not."

It is interesting to note that most of the managers we work with who have been described as angry or moody are well aware that these emotions are affecting their personal and professional lives. Someone with a ton of guts has told these managers that their responses to situations are wrong and undermine morale. However, the managers continue to use these behaviors in the workplace.

The challenge with being labeled as moody, angry, or as displaying emotions that do not fit the situation, is that people are unsure of how to approach the person for fear of how he will respond. People walk around the halls asking each other, "How is he today?" Or, "Is today a good day?" Being considered a moody or emotional person is one of the toughest labels to shed and change in the minds of employees and peers.

Stupid Behavior #2: Impulsive Decisions

Some emotional managers tend to be reactive and are known for making impulsive decisions. These managers accumulate a track record for making quick decisions that undermine the organization's success. Managers who are guilty of shooting without first taking aim are fond of screaming "Fire, fire, fire!" Once they sound the alarm, they stand back to watch the troops rally to put out the blaze.

We recently worked with an impulsive vice president (VP) of facilities who had a strong dislike for the smell of burned popcorn. Being a decisive leader, she banned microwave popcorn throughout the facility.

Despite her policy, twice in the previous month she had detected the offending odor. Wanting to solve this major crisis, this VP dedicated the efforts of her entire facilities team to researching, purchasing, and installing video surveillance cameras in the break rooms. Her efforts didn't stop there. She then assigned team members on a rotating basis to review the surveillance tapes. Last we heard, the popcorn burner had not been identified, but the search continues.

Typically, after the fire has been put out, the workforce resumes working on its organizational priorities. People feel good about their accomplishments, but it doesn't take long for the impulsive manager to stumble upon another crisis and once again sound the alarm. With a unanimous "not again," the entire team drops what it was doing and rallies to put out yet another fire. Enlightened team members view the "crisis of the day" as being both preventable and a major disruption to their work and overall organizational objectives.

We worked at a company where the CEO had a personal dislike for the head of an important project that impacted the entire organization. Being known for his impulsive decisions, the CEO determined that this person should be fired that day. When we asked the CEO what his plan was when the project manager was fired, he looked at us and said, "I don't have a plan." Then he asked, "Do you know where we could find someone who is qualified?"

These emotional and impulsive managers share a common characteristic. While known for their decisiveness, they are also known for their self-centered crisis-management leadership style. They seldom consider overall organizational or departmental priorities, and they hold little regard for the importance of someone else's work.

Stupid Behavior #3: Blaming Others

Number three on our list of behaviors that get managers into big trouble is not taking initiative to proactively solve problems and produce results that lead to the organization's success. These managers are famous for blaming their lack of results on other departments, their direct reports, their bosses, and even customers.

But there is an exception to this rule. When things go right, these managers are almost always the first to accept the credit and praise.

These managers are famous for focusing all their energy on answering two questions. The first question is, "What is wrong?" The second question is, "Who is to blame?" The managers who reach a whole new level address a third question, which is: "Who do I psychologically whack or punish?"

> When you lack confidence in your ability to influence your environment and take the necessary actions to produce positive results, one way to compensate is to look for others to blame for your own inadequacies.

Psychological whacks occur when a manager talks about what is wrong with a person or another department or a situation. And the talking always occurs behind their backs. These managers never have the guts to address the issue directly with the individual.

We served as executive coaches to two high-level, highly compensated managers who refused to cooperate with one other, spoke negatively about their rival's department with their own team members, consistently gossiped about the other, and pointed fingers at each other for their difficulties. In fact, sometimes it seemed that each manager was spending a full day strategically plotting the demise of the other. Ultimately, despite coaching and a fair amount of warning, both individuals lost their jobs due to their inability to look for solutions to their conflict.

After years of working with executives who have difficulty maintaining effective workplace relationships while blaming others for their inadequacies, we most often found that, if we dug deep into their methods of operation, we discovered that they lacked confidence in their ability to get the job done. When you lack confidence in your ability to influence your environment and take the necessary actions to produce positive results, one way to compensate is to look for others to blame for your own inadequacies.

Stupid Behavior #4: It's All About Me!

These are the managers who sound like they are warming up for an opera as they sing praises of "me, me, me, my, my, my, and I, I, I." These managers love to tell you about their amazing prior accomplishments and how the organizations they worked for in the past were so wonderful.

By relating their great achievements, they indirectly put people, and their current organization, down in order to build themselves up. The way things were done in the past is often an opportunity for them to speak derogatorily about everyone else.

We interviewed a manager who was adamant that not one person in the company had the knowledge or skills to accomplish the company's goals. We were stunned by this comment and asked the manager to be sure we understood him correctly, "Not one person has either the knowledge or skills?" This manager boldly responded, "No, I am the only one in the organization with the big picture."

It is one thing to lead change and take an organization to an even higher level. The highest-ranked leaders in the Benchmarks define a clear, compelling vision; clarify performance expectations; and then communicate these goals to staff. It is another thing, however, to attempt to motivate people to change by telling them how badly they handled things in the past. That approach does nothing but cause animosity and resentment toward the manager.

In an interview to collect feedback on a manager, one employee pointed out: "We have been successful enough to hire this new manager and move him and his family all the way across the country. To have him join our organization and, in the first month, listen to him tell everyone how bad we are and how good he is just turns people off. You are here as consultants because this manager was hit by friendly fire."

Managers who take all the credit for the department's, division's, or organization's success show a second form of "it's all about me." In taking all the credit, they find it difficult to praise, recognize, or give credit to the people who actually did the work that led to the success. One of the managers we coached confidently said, "My boss has no idea what I do. If it weren't for me, the company would have wasted thousands of dollars buying needless equipment."

We don't know about the equipment, but the executive was being coached because his employees were caught in a revolving door. None stayed for any length of time and the last few, on the way out, had alleged that he was egotistical and arrogant.

Stupid Behavior #5: If You Think Today Is Bad, Just Wait!

Although rare, from time to time we conduct employee opinion surveys where we find the opinions of the management team are more negative than the opinions of the employees. We uncover this issue with the statement, "This organization has an exciting future." A second statement that helps to uncover employees' feelings regarding the future is, "My organization offers me the type of job I will want three years from now." In the situations where employees' opinions are higher than those of the management team, we feel like telling the managers to turn over control of the company to employees because they have an even more positive view of the organization's future than the managers do.

There is a reason why a compelling, positive vision of the future is the foundation for Best-of-the-Best organizations. With negative visions come low aspirations. If managers don't think the situation can be improved (vision), then they do not raise their levels of aspirations or set goals to improve the situation. Poor visions with mediocre goals lead to a workforce with low morale.

If you are a manager who has a negative vision combined with low aspirations for improvement, the greatest gift you can give to both yourself and the organization is to quit.

Stupid Behavior #6: Now What We Have Here Is a Failure to Communicate

In 1967, Paul Newman starred in a great movie, *Cool Hand Luke*. In this classic, Luke is sent to a prison camp for cutting the heads off of parking meters. When asked why he would do such a thing, the only explanation he gives is, "Small town, not much to do in the evenin'." But the greatest quote comes later in the movie when Strother Martin tells Paul Newman: "Now what we have here is a failure to communicate."

This insightful statement is applicable to managers who don't appropriately communicate, and, in turn, single-handedly undermine workplace excellence. There are several categories of communication blunders, including communication that is not timely, direct, or honest.

Recently, in analyzing an organization's employee opinion survey data, there were large discrepancies in response to the statement, "Managers and supervisors at my company seek the opinions and thoughts of the employees who work here." As outsiders viewing the culture from the employees' perspective, it was clear to us that some managers asked for their employees' ideas and opinions while others didn't. We also noted that, in general, when responses to this and other statements about communication were more favorable within a department, scores throughout the whole survey likewise were higher. In other words, when people were asked for their insights and felt that their input was valued, they tended to be more positive about their relationship with their employer.

We gained insight into that company's organizational climate regarding employee input and innovation when one senior level manager said, "Just because we ask, it doesn't necessarily mean we will take action on their input. They have to understand that we've been at this business for a long time and know what works and what doesn't."

Here is a sure-fire recipe for failure: Assume that you know more than your employees and that they don't need to know anything other than how to do their jobs. Just tell employees what you think they need to hear and then sit back and try to have fun when the negative surprises start rising to your level!

This is referred to as The Mushroom Theory of Management. These managers believe that if you keep employees in the dark and feed them a load of manure, like mushrooms, they will do just fine.

Then there are the managers who are too busy for timely communication. They are so active keeping all the balls in the air they feel they do not have time to communicate necessary information that would keep customers happy and employees successful. Because they feel everything is faster if they just do it themselves, they do not delegate. In haste, they cover up one mess only to create another because of the lack of communication. People in the organization are continually surprised because they find things out at the last minute or after the fact, when they cannot positively impact the outcome.

Another example of this stupid behavior is the failure to provide direct and honest feedback. These managers go around telling everyone what they are thinking *except* for the person who actually could do something with the information. In interviews, we love to ask the question, "Have you told your employees, boss, or peers that you have strong concerns about the way this project is progressing?" It is not uncommon for a manager who is struggling in the organization to look us in the eye and hesitantly say, "No."

When we push managers on why there has not been direct communication, we hear the following excuses: they feel the feedback would not be appreciated; it is outside their scope of authority to give honest feedback; or, our favorite, "I was hoping they would figure it out and change without me needing to say anything."

Some managers will actually lie when providing information or when directly asked a question. It is almost impossible to build a relationship where people willingly follow you when you are perceived to be untrustworthy. We worked with an organization where, at an all-employee meeting, one person asked the CEO if there was going to be a layoff. The CEO, who had been working diligently with the senior management on executing the layoff at the end of the month, looked at all the employees and said, "No, it is not in my plans to do a layoff."

This was a lie. As hard as it is to tell employees that their jobs may be jeopardized by a layoff, the honest thing to say would be, "As difficult as it is for me to talk about something as devastating as a layoff, I need you to know that a layoff is a very real possibility. My commitment to you is to communicate information to you as soon as we have specific numbers and a concrete plan of how we will take care of our people who are laid off."

What is fascinating about people who do not consistently speak the truth is that when they want to really emphasize a point, they insert the phrase, "I am going to be honest with you." Sometimes they even ask, "Can I be honest with you?" or "Can I be frank?" Every time we hear these words we feel like saying, "We are glad you are going to make this conversation special by being honest. Does this mean that you haven't been honest before?"

Stupid Behavior #7: Blessed With Two Ears and One Mouth

The old saying God gave us two ears and only one mouth and intended us to use them in that given proportion is applicable here. Managers who undermine workplace excellence have a tendency to talk first, and listen later. A lot later—and sometimes not at all.

Not listening or asking questions to gain even more information is like walking into your doctor's office and saying, "Doctor, I really hurt and need your help." The doctor responds, "As a doctor for over thirty years, I am one of the best at helping people get better. Here is a prescription. Take four of the pills each day for ten days. At the end of ten days, you will feel better. Any questions?" Any patient with brains would have to be thinking: "You don't want to know where I hurt, how long I have hurt, or what have I done to try to make the hurt go away?"

One summer, I (Peter) went to the pharmacy to buy pain-relief medication for my youngest daughter who was stung by a bee. Because she was only seven-years-old and I wasn't confident about what to buy, I went up to the pharmacist, held up the Benadryl, and said, "My daughter was stung by a bee. Would this be a good thing for my daughter to take?" Without any thought, the pharmacist replied,

"Yeah, it should work." I walked away, shaking my head and thinking, *She didn't even ask questions like: "How old is your daughter? Is she allergic to bees? How long ago was she stung? How much swelling does she have? Where was she stung?* In my opinion, this pharmacist committed a form of malpractice.

In reality, many managers commit leadership malpractice on a daily basis because they react without thinking and say something they later regret. Instead of opening their mouths and moving closer to their goals, they open their mouths and say something that moves them farther away from their goals. They should have been asking questions and listening.

There are a few reasons these managers do not listen well. First, they do not feel they need to know new or additional information or that the new information will help them be better managers. Second, managers who do not actively listen believe they already know the answers. And third, managers who do not listen feel a strong need to control the conversation by doing all the talking.

These three reasons are powerful enough for many managers to lose the desire to be great listeners. Without the desire to listen, the impact on the manager's colleagues is almost always the same. If given the choice, people would prefer not to work with the manager.

> ### TIP
> Looking to improve your listening skills (or those of someone you know)? Go to www.peterstark.com, and enter the word ENGAGE in the Tip Box.

Stupid Behavior #8: Please Like Me, I Want To Be Your Friend

One of the behaviors that gets managers into huge trouble is working hard to be friends with coworkers, or only doing things they think others in the organization will like. Recently, we asked a supervisor if she had coached an employee who was coming to work late and not meeting the standards of her job. This supervisor responded with, "No. I have not talked with her about her performance because we are good friends."

We were dumbfounded. What kind of true friend would exhibit behaviors like chronic tardiness and poor performance, which would undermine her supervisor/friend's ability to be successful in her role? Undermining your supervisor/friend's success at work is a twisted characteristic of friendship.

Recognizing and rewarding excellent performance is a key practice for organizations in the Best-of-the-Best Benchmark. Managers who let a real or perceived friendship get in the way of identifying perform-ance problems that affect the entire team are not likely to achieve the organization's vision. They are more likely to demoralize their most productive workers and lose them.

In another organization, a supervisor told us that he did not give people honest feedback because he really cared about his direct reports and wanted them to like him as their supervisor. When super-visors tell us about not being honest with people because of their enormous need to be liked, we are reminded of the story of the old man, the young boy, and the donkey.

An old man and a young boy were walking a donkey down the highway. A car stopped and the driver told the old man, "This is crazy. You have a young boy walking with you and he should be riding on the perfectly healthy donkey." So the old man, in an attempt to make the driver happy, put the boy on the donkey and started walking again.

A little farther down the road, another car pulled over and a man said to the old man, "This is crazy. The young boy is perfectly healthy. You are an old man. You should be riding the donkey." In an attempt to please the person, the old man took the boy off the donkey, climbed up, and they started walking once again.

They had not been walking but a few minutes when another car slowed down and the driver stated to the old man, "The donkey is perfectly capable of carrying both of you. Both of you should be riding the donkey." Once again, the pleasing old man lifted the young boy aboard and they both went down the street riding the donkey.

Next, the donkey walked up to a creek but would not step foot in the water. Another passerby stopped and told the old man that he needed to get off and pull the donkey into the creek. He did so, but the donkey would not budge. Someone else stopped by and told them that both the old man and the boy needed to tug the donkey. This passerby even described the donkey as a stubborn teenager. Still yet, another person told the old man that the boy needed to pull and the old man needed to push the donkey into the water.

Lastly, one sage who was the owner of many donkeys told the old man that both the old man and the boy needed to get behind the donkey and push with all their might and once in the water, the donkey would grudgingly walk to the other side. They took the latest advice to please the sage and pushed so hard that the donkey stumbled into the creek, broke his neck, and drowned.

There is a moral to this story that applies to leadership. If you try to please everyone, you are going to lose your ass.

Stupid Behavior #9: Exhibiting Poor Judgment

"What were you thinking?"

That is our favorite question to ask managers we are coaching who have been accused of exercising incredibly poor judgment. So what constitutes poor judgment? Here are a few examples.

Managers show poor judgment when they:

Talk negatively about one employee in front of another employee. When managers do this, they think they are confiding in one employee and indirectly building an even stronger relationship with the employee they are speaking to. The reality is that any time a manager speaks poorly about one employee to another employee, the person walks away thinking, "If he talks this nasty about others behind their backs, then what does he say about me when I am not present?"

Speak negatively about their boss or organization. Talk about biting the hand that feeds you! As a manager confides to others about how stupid the boss can be, the listeners are thinking the boss must be stupid for hiring someone who is not loyal and talks behind people's backs. It has been our experience that people who talk negatively about their boss or their organization eventually are asked to leave by that very boss.

Believe that direct reports have a desire to become personally involved in a relationship with them, and then act on these desires. We are the first to admit that many personal relationships began in a working environment. Unfortunately, the problem with becoming emotionally involved with a subordinate is that it creates tremendous liabilities for the manager, the employee, and the organization.

Use foul language or say inappropriate things to others. Although many of us may have been guilty of slipping occasionally, it's important to recognize that foul language will work against you in a business environment.

Stupid Behavior #10: Tell Me Only What I Want To Hear!

Defensive managers tend to surround themselves with "yes" men and women. They do not appreciate feedback that does not support what they believe. These managers do not value the truth. They may respond with an emotional outburst of anger, tell the communicant why the message is wrong, start the silent treatment, or exclude the team member from the manager's selected group of people who are allowed to give feedback.

The outcome of being defensive is that these managers produce an environment where they do not have a good grasp of reality and make decisions without having all the available information. This vicious cycle starts because people do not feel comfortable sharing important information when they know that the manager won't agree with the information that needs to be conveyed.

For instance, in the interview phase of an executive coaching project, we were getting a consistent theme from employees. In a

> ## "It seems like if enough people tell you that you have a tail, you ought to turn around and take a look!"

variety of different ways, employees were telling us that their boss was rude. When asked for examples, we heard things like: "He cuts you off when you're speaking to him." "He hangs up on you." "He walks right by you, sees you, and doesn't even say 'hello'." "He asks you a question and turns around and leaves before you are finished talking." One bold employee even said, "We've tried talking to him about this. He doesn't want to know. It seems like if enough people tell you that you have a tail, you ought to turn around and take a look!"

We loved the employee's advice! Managers who exhibit this stupid behavior just don't want to know reality or don't want to be confused by another point of view.

Stupid Behavior #11: Not Trusting People

It is amazing how many managers hire good people and then don't trust them to get the job done. Managers who do not trust people don't like to delegate because they feel a need to personally complete anything of importance. This belief becomes a self-fulfilling prophecy.

If you do not trust people, then you do not delegate. If you do not delegate, then you do not develop your team members' skills to handle even greater responsibility. When people do not gain experience because you do not delegate, you confirm your initial belief that they cannot be trusted.

Whether you believe you can or cannot trust people, you are right. Employees who believe that their boss trusts them go out of their way to demonstrate discretionary effort, which ensures they do not undermine the expectations and trust of their boss. If managers believe they cannot trust people and, hence, do not delegate, they are also right. The employees do not have the necessary skills to fulfill the manager's expectations.

There is a second problem that emerges when managers do not trust team members. It does not take long before the staff does not trust the manager. This happens because people think, "I am a good and trustworthy person. I deserve to be communicated to, delegated to, and to assume even greater responsibility." When the manager does not do this, direct reports start to believe that they cannot trust their manager. The direct reports start to withhold information and the lack-of-trust-cycle begins to grow.

Also under the umbrella of not trusting people is a desperate need to control everything. If these managers are not in total control, they are not comfortable. They worry that if someone else does the job and it is not perfect, they will either not be able to fix the problem or it will reflect negatively on them. To maintain this high degree of control, these managers do not:

- Communicate necessary information in a timely manner, if at all.
- Delegate tasks to build up the capacity of both people and their organization.
- Schedule vacations because without them being there controlling everything, it will all fall apart or, worse, everyone will figure out that this control freak is not needed.

FREQUENCY—THE NAME OF THE GAME

Why do managers exhibit these stupid behaviors? While reading this chapter, there's a good chance you nodded (and maybe laughed) in recognition. The longer your career has been, the more likely it is that you have encountered these types of behaviors.

The difference is that poor managers choose to follow one or more of these behaviors frequently and, in some cases, to an extreme degree. Even when their peers, staff, and an executive coach ask questions and provide feedback to improve their leadership skills, they do not change the behaviors. It's a losing game.

Other managers are willing to learn and practice new approaches. They decide to develop a game plan that will improve their personal leadership skills and, consequently, the performance of their team and the organization itself.

We believe that it is possible to stop stupid behaviors and replace them with positive leadership skills. In the next chapter, you'll learn how to do this from the Best-of-the-Best.

Think about your boss and answer the questions on this pop quiz. For each of the questions, base your response on a period of time. Do not generate your answer based on just one incident or action. We all slip and do something stupid from time to time. What gets managers in trouble is consistently doing stupid things.

STUPID BEHAVIORS OF MANAGERS—A POP QUIZ		
1. **True** False		My boss is a pessimist. He/she truly believes the glass is half empty today and that tomorrow will most likely be worse, not better, than today.
2. **True** False		My boss is moody. I never know exactly what mood he/she is going to be in or what the response will be to my request.
3. **True** False		My boss has a temper. When he/she is angry, everyone knows it.
4. **True** False		My boss blames others for his/her own lack of responsibility and/or action.
5. **True** False		My boss does not trust his/her direct reports.
6. **True** False		My boss withholds necessary information from subordinates and other departments until he/she is forced to reveal the information.
7. **True** False		My boss lies or clouds the truth if he/she feels it will help accomplish his/her goals.
8. **True** False		My boss speaks poorly about his/her boss.
9. **True** False		My boss has a clique of people in the department and in the company that he/she likes and listens to. You are either in his/her group or you are not.

Continued next page

10. **True**	**False**	My boss speaks derogatorily about one direct report in front of other direct reports.
11. **True**	**False**	My boss uses foul language in front of others in the organization.
12. **True**	**False**	My boss says things that are clearly inappropriate in a business environment (jokes comments about race, gender, dress, appearance, sexual orientation, sexual desires or content).
13. **True**	**False**	My boss does not care about my personal or professional goals.
14. **True**	**False**	My boss is a poor listener.
15. **True**	**False**	My boss can take a minor problem and make a mountain out of a molehill. Everyone in the department/company feels the pain.
16. **True**	**False**	My boss does not delegate full responsibility and authority to me to do my job.
17. **True**	**False**	My boss does not publicly praise people when they do a great job.
18. **True**	**False**	My boss loves to personally take the credit for our organization's success.
19. **True**	**False**	My boss publicly talks about other's lack of intelligence, or takes pride in pointing out people who have different opinions and in his/her eyes "don't get it."
20. **True**	**False**	My boss has a difficult time admitting when he/she is wrong or makes a mistake.

Scoring: Give your boss five points for every statement you scored as true. The lower your boss's score on the pop quiz, the higher the odds that you like your boss and love your job. The higher your boss's score on the pop quiz, the more difficult it likely is for you to do your job and work for this person. (If your boss scored over 90%, we would welcome your e-mail detailing one of your boss's stupid behaviors. Send your experience to peter@pbsconsulting.com. We love great stories. There's always the opportunity to include your tale in our next book.)

Twelve-Step Recovery from Stupid Behaviors

It seems obvious, but it is worth stating: It's vital to recover from stupid behaviors. Companies with higher levels of engaged employees are more productive and more likely to retain qualified, top-performing staff members. As a result, their organizations are more competitive and more successful.

It is also important to emphasize again that every manager has done, or said, something in a working environment and then thought, "That was stupid." Although some of the behaviors managers exhibit can severely and negatively impact people in the organization, we strongly believe there is hope for these managers.

Remember, the highest-rated leaders in the Benchmarks were twenty-six points higher than the lowest-rated managers when their employees were asked about their ability to admit a mistake. Great leaders are comfortable admitting a mistake and then moving forward to make things better.

You can develop your skills as a leader and increase your value to the organization by following the twelve steps outlined below. You will mitigate the impact of past stupid manager behaviors and lay a foundation on which to build successful future relationships.

Step #1: Stop the Behavior

Although stopping sounds so easy, we have found that lifelong behaviors are some of the most difficult things to change. We recently worked with a newly hired CEO who was charged with changing the culture of a fifty-year-old financial institution. The average length of service for employees was over fifteen years. Keeping employees with this much experience was the good news. The bad news was that it was much more difficult to implement change into the existing culture.

This CEO, who suffered from Stupid Behavior #4, "It's All About Me," continually boasted about all the marvelous things he had done in his career and how lucky everyone was that he had decided to take this job. He reminded everyone that he "had several offers even better than this one." To add insult to injury, this CEO continually put down the entire management team by repeatedly saying things like, "You people really have no clue what great customer service looks like." Another insult the CEO loved to lob to the entire executive team was, "There is not one mid-level manager in this organization who is capable of becoming a senior vice president."

Not surprisingly, these comments destroyed morale not only for the mid-level managers, but also for the executives who were convinced this CEO talked nastily about them as well. We coached this CEO on several occasions about the importance of not putting down either individuals or groups in public. Each time we met, we reminded the CEO that this behavior destroys morale and he would achieve better results by saying "we" versus "you people" and focusing on building a positive future as a team versus putting down the past. But the CEO never stopped exhibiting this stupid behavior. When he was finally asked to leave two years into his tenure, he left saying,

"Not one member of the board had the guts to stand up to these whiny employees."

Changing behaviors is hard. It takes patience, commitment, and unwavering perseverance.

Step #2: Admit You Made a Mistake

If you commit one of the eleven stupid behaviors, don't make excuses. Quickly come clean and tell people, "I messed up. Here is my plan to fix my stupid action. If anyone has another suggestion for improvement for me, please tell me." Or, "This time I really called that wrong. I should have listened to what you were trying to tell me. I've learned from this mistake and will do things differently next time."

Whether you made a mistake in a personal or professional relationship, acknowledging when you did so is a powerful step. This is one of the key ways a leader can make a difference. As was stated before, when you are willing to admit a mistake, people are likely to forgive you.

Step #3: Apologize

When you have done something that has had a negative impact on someone else, say, "I am sorry that what I did impacted you that way."

We worked with a senior VP who became angry in a department meeting and started to shout and swear while pounding his fist on the table. The senior VP then abruptly ended the meeting and walked out. Needless to say, the department staff was a little quiet for the rest of the day.

Later in the day, the senior VP called another department meeting. Some team members thought they were being re-grouped for a second ambush. Instead, he sat down and said, "This is going to be a short meeting. I want everyone to know that what I did this morning was uncalled for. I have felt terrible all day that I lost my cool. I totally misdirected my anger and I want everyone to know I am really sorry." The manager went on to add, "When I thought about why I lost my cool, it is because I don't know how to fix this problem. I am asking for your help."

With those statements the manager became a leader. The meeting that was supposed to be over in five minutes went on for another hour, with most of the team members contributing solutions to solve the problem.

Often, when we serve as executive coaches for managers who have been accused of doing something inappropriate in the workplace, it is apparent that the situation escalated because the managers would not own their actions and apologize. We often hear this justification: "I won't apologize because I didn't do anything wrong. They just took it wrong and overreacted. I'm not going to apologize because that would be admitting guilt, and I'm not guilty."

Yet in 99% of these scenarios, if the manager possessed the confidence and emotional maturity to genuinely say, "I'm sorry. I apologize for what happened and how it made you feel. It won't happen again," the situation would have been over and never escalated to the point where mediation was needed to resolve the dispute.

In real life, when someone admits she made a mistake and apologizes sincerely, it makes it much more difficult to stay angry with her. When managers summon the courage to admit a mistake and have the guts to apologize, we are convinced that they are much less likely to be hit by friendly fire and far more likely to build trust and morale levels in the workplace.

People understand mistakes but retain little respect for managers who won't own their behaviors and apologize for the impact of their actions on others.

Step #4: Ask for Help

Some managers view asking for help as a sign of weakness or lack of confidence. Exactly the opposite is true. Asking for help from your boss, your direct reports, your peers, or even a coach is a sign of confidence and strength and will help to increase your chances for success. It is important to realize that most people want you to be successful and when you ask for help, you can increase your chances of achieving success. The tips below will help you to get the assistance you need, when you need it.

First, ask early in the process. Waiting until the last minute becomes stressful for everyone. Rather than being motivated to help you achieve your goal, the person you are asking may even become resentful of your request.

Second, be specific in your request for help. The more exact you are, the better your odds of getting help that is beneficial to achieving your goal.

Third, give people a specific time frame for the help to be provided. Without a definite deadline, managers can end up doing the task on their own, even after they asked for aid, because no one knew when the help was needed. This can also create an environment where people lose the desire to assist the manager in the future.

> **TIP**
>
> Interested in building your confidence or the confidence of someone on your team? Go to www.peterstark.com, and enter the word ENGAGE in the Tip Box.

Step #5: Give Credit Where Credit Is Due

Confident managers feel comfortable giving praise and recognizing people for their contributions to the organization's success. The more genuine praise and recognition you give people, the more they will be motivated to help you, and the organization, achieve success.

While most managers spend a considerable amount of time thinking about workplace challenges and attempting to find solutions, great leaders also invest time thinking about what is going well and looking for opportunities to recognize and reward people for their positive contributions. The majority (86.7%) of the employees at the Best-of-the-Best organizations felt that "I receive credit and recognition when I do a good job." Their managers' attitudes are "It's all about them."

Step #6: Take Responsibility

When the results are not what people expected, don't complain, blame, or explain. Instead, take responsibility to correct the problem. This is not the same thing as admitting you caused the problem. Most likely, you did not cause the problem.

What most organizations need are managers who focus 100% of their energy on correcting the problem and taking responsibility to ensure the results are in alignment with the organization's goals.

> When the results are not what people expected, don't complain, blame, or explain.

Great leaders truly believe that the gift they bring to the organization is the willingness to take responsibility to ensure the organization achieves the best outcomes. When challenges arise, their responses are, "What went wrong? How are we going to fix it? What did we learn from this? What will we do to ensure this doesn't happen again in the future?"

When you answer these questions, you and your team can solve the problem. At the same time, you can identify the processes or performance gaps that may have led to the problem and fix these, too. You can maintain accountability and avoid the stupid behavior of blaming others.

Step #7: Focus on the Future

Managers who are famous for blaming others when things do not go as planned almost always focus on the past. The fastest way out of this trap is to focus on the future by asking these two questions: Where do we want to be? How do we get there?

Most people will drop their Cover Your Assets (CYA) mentality and pitch in to help solve problems if the discussion is focused on creating a positive future. You already know that key number one and the first step to becoming a great leader is a positive and compelling vision of the future.

Step #8: Take Action

Procrastination leads to serious problems for managers. Most managers know what is right and what they need to do. Managers who do stupid things make excuses for not taking action and doing what everyone knows needs to be done.

You are the role model for your team. To borrow a slogan from Nike, "Just do it."

If you suffer from "T.N.T." disease (I'll do it ... Tomorrow, Not Today), chances are your team is suffering, too. Prioritize, create a realistic plan for getting your work accomplished, and then work your plan. No excuses. Just do it!

Step #9: Think First and Then Speak

I don't know about you, but I (Peter) cannot give constructive feedback when I am angry or upset. It does not matter whether the situation involves my wife, my children, or an employee. When I am angry, my word choice is not effective in helping me move closer to my goal. So, if you are like me, what do you do? The best thing is to think about the situation and respond to your counterpart when you are emotionally calm.

During a coaching session, a manager who had gotten himself into trouble for responding defensively to a difficult employee said, "What people need to understand is that I get mad. I yell. Then, it's off my chest and I'm over it." I said, "Yes. It's off your chest. It's on someone else's chest. That's what got you into trouble." He said, "They need to just get over it." I said, "They didn't. That's why you are here."

Finally, he responded with, "I think this may be the most important thing I've learned so far in our work together. I can get over what I do, but it has a lasting impact on others. I need to think about what I say before I say it." This is a terrific example of a manager recovering from a stupid behavior!

Some managers have told us that the philosophy of not communicating at the moment is not being honest. Honesty is wonderful. We are in full support of frank communication. But it is important to note that the words that come out of your mouth are permanent. If you can communicate when you are angry and are able to move closer to your long-term goals, then go for it. If your communication when you are angry moves you farther away from your goals, think first, and then speak.

Step #10: Listen and Ask Questions

As our 88-year-old dad is so fond of saying, "People like you a whole lot better when they are talking." It's so simple and so true. Get others to speak first. You can learn so much more about leadership when you listen.

After your counterparts are finished talking, ask them open-ended questions to gain even more information and further clarification. Be like a doctor who asks all the necessary questions so you can write an accurate prescription when you do finally open your mouth to speak.

There's a very good reason why you should ask questions before you articulate your position. The most highly rated managers rate twenty-three percentage points higher on the scale when employees say they solicit opinions on work within their areas of responsibility.

Step #11: Thank People

Please and *thank you* are words that go a long way in building or re-building strong relationships after a manager does something stupid. *Thank you* is especially helpful when people give you feedback that either you did not want to hear or was difficult for the other person to share with you.

Recently, I (Jane) conducted a telephone seminar. At the conclusion, a participant e-mailed to let me know he felt that a point I made—"Great managers keep their people uncomfortable"—was bad. I thought about e-mailing the gentleman back to explain in more detail why I feel that this is an important concept for managers to understand and practice.

Instead, I e-mailed the participant and thanked him for caring enough about me as a presenter to share his feedback. Then I asked him for more details on why he felt my advice was inappropriate. He e-mailed me back an additional two pages of clarifying feedback. After reading the additional two pages, I realized that he agreed with about 99% of what I said. There was one small point he disagreed with.

After he shared his example supporting his disagreement, I e-mailed him again and told him that based on his unique example, I agreed with him. Thanking people and getting even more information is a great strategy.

Step #12: **Be Grateful**

One way to be grateful is to imagine coming to work tomorrow and finding that none of your employees have shown up. What would you do? There is no way you can run the whole department or organization all by yourself. If no one is following you, then you are not a leader. If you are going to be successful as a manager, you need people.

In the words of Brian Tracy, "Develop an attitude of gratitude, and give thanks for everything that happens to you, knowing that every step forward is a step toward achieving something bigger and better than your current situation." Be grateful you:

- Are employed
- Have customers
- Have a team who needs you
- Have a loving family and friends
- Have a supervisor who values your contribution
- Are in this position because you can make a difference
- Are alive!

MOVE FORWARD INTO A POSITIVE LEADERSHIP ROLE

About 50% of the managers we coach who have been accused of exhibiting stupid behaviors turn their reputations around and become positive managers and role models in their organizations. You might ask, what happens to the other 50%?

The other 50% exhibit what we call "Popeye Syndrome." Popeye, the famous cartoon character, is famous for saying, "I'm Popeye the Sailor Man. I am what I am and that's all that I am." He is an interesting role model for managers who exhibit stupid behaviors.

Is there any cure for "Popeye Syndrome?" Yes. Popeye also demonstrated the ability to recover. After eating a can of spinach, he could overcome any obstacle and no barrier was too large. He is an inspiring role model for the manager who says, "I can learn from, change, and fix these past stupid mistakes. Watch me go!"

You can recover from stupid behaviors and replace them with the leadership skills exhibited by the highest-rated managers. You can start right now.

PART THREE

Create
Workplace
Excellence

6

The 76 Strategies

Are you a leader who inspires innovative thinking and top performance? If you are not, The 10 Keys to Workplace Excellence will open new ways to engage employees and build an army of loyal customers. Even better, the ten keys previously outlined align with the seventy-six strategies described in this chapter, which are used by companies in the Best-of-the-Best Benchmark.

We know that there are some natural leaders, but most of us need to continually learn or refresh our management skills. It's inspiring to remember that about half of the managers we coach make changes and move forward as higher-performing leaders. The seventy-six strategies, with examples of how the Best-of-the-Best leaders put them into practice, will help you do the same thing.

Day after day, your actions create your work environment. That doesn't mean that you suddenly need to put all seventy-six strategies into action at once. It will benefit you and your team to start implementing them with the same strategic vision you apply to your organization's product. One leader can make a tremendous difference—either positive or negative. Are you a leader who exhibits and inspires the spirit of workplace excellence as you walk through the door? If not, here is what you can do.

KEY # 1: A COMPELLING, POSITIVE VISION WITH CLEAR GOALS

There is a reason why a compelling, positive vision is the first key to workplace excellence. How can you get there if you don't know where you are going? Ninety percent of employees at the Best-of-the-Best organizations understand their company's goals. But the clearest vision in the world will only be effective if it's communicated to employees, and if everyone's actions—including senior managers'—strive to fulfill the vision.

Strategy 1. Communicate your organization's purpose

Purpose is a powerful motivator that clearly defines your organization's reason for existence. It answers the question "Why?" rather than simply explaining what you do and how you do it. Your purpose, when clearly articulated, explains from your customer's viewpoint what your business is. For example, our company is a management-consulting firm whose purpose is clear. We are focused on helping our clients create an environment where employees love to come to work and customers love to do business. We align every service we provide and every product we produce with this purpose. Examples of some well-known organizations with clear purposes are listed below:

- Starbucks—committed to being premier purveyor of the finest coffee in the world.
- 3M—solve unsolved problems innovatively.
- Disney—make people happy.

- Mary Kay—offer women unlimited opportunities.
- Merck—provide society with superior products and services by developing innovations and solutions that improve the quality of life.
- Southwest Airlines—dedication to the highest quality of customer service delivered with a sense of warmth, friendliness, individual pride, and company spirit.

What purpose or higher cause drives your team or organization? Employees tend to raise their motivation and productivity to a higher level when a clear purpose or higher cause channels their work. Every employee on your team needs to understand how your organization's purpose and their individual actions contribute to your organization's success. To remain motivated, loyal, and enthusiastic, people need to be connected to a meaningful purpose. Clearly identify and communicate your purpose loudly and often.

Clearly identify and communicate your purpose loudly and often.

> "A leader has the vision and conviction that a dream can be achieved. He inspires the power and energy to get it done."
>
> **RALPH LAUREN**

Strategy 2. **Get excited about tomorrow**

George Burns once said, "Every morning, the first thing I do is get up and read the obituary section of the newspaper. If my name is not in there, it is going to be a great day." George Burns was also the person who scheduled a performance at the London Palladium on his one-hundredth birthday. That is a powerful positive vision of the future. One day, someone asked Burns how long he felt he was going to live. Burns replied, "How can I die? I'm booked." Although Burns did not make the concert at the London Palladium, he did live to celebrate his one-hundred birthday.

Are you a glass-half-full or a glass-half-empty type of leader? Some people you work with can make both work and life seem like a chore. I (Jane) once asked an unhappy employee why he stayed at an organization. He responded, "Six years, five months, and four days until I retire." That response sounds more like a prison sentence than a career. But he does get to go home at night for a conjugal visit. What is sad is that we believe this individual is, most likely, not excited about his personal life, either. It is very difficult to say, "I hate my job, but at 5:00 PM, I become excited about my life." Life doesn't work that way.

The best way to be excited about tomorrow is to have things to do. We are excited about:

- Developing our next book.
- Guiding the executives we are working with to become more successful leaders.
- Helping our staff grow.
- Taking our firm to the next level.
- Watching our teenagers, who know everything, grow up, go to college, and move out of the house!

What are you excited about? What do you love about life, your career, and your organization? What is on your to-do list? To be excited about coming to work each day—because you love what you do and who you work with—promotes workplace excellence. When you really love what you do it is not just a job. Leaders who are excited about tomorrow attract more followers who are motivated to accomplish the organization's goals.

"Anything's possible if you've got enough nerve."
J. K. ROWLING

Strategy 3. **Have high expectations**

When it comes to change in organizations, there is no greater resistance than in the field of education. If not proven in theory and written about in books, then educators do not see a reason to change. However, a few renegade school districts are changing the paradigm in the business of education.

The Poway Unified School District (PUSD) in Poway, California, is rated as one of the top districts in the country for kindergarten through twelfth grade. For more than twenty-five years, PUSD had the same superintendent, who built a national reputation for excellence. We are convinced that home prices in this district are inflated by an extra $200,000 to $300,000 because of the school's reputation. When you have a reputation this strong, you focus on maintaining what you have rather than taking your success to a higher level.

In 2001, PUSD hired a new superintendent, Don Phillips, to lead the district. When you inherit a success, how you make it better is a major concern. In the last decade, most school districts have transitioned from a vision of "Every child can learn" to "Every child will learn." The second vision, "Every child will learn," holds the district and its employees more accountable for the educational success of every child. When Phillips and his cabinet came together, they formed a new vision that took "Every child will learn" to a higher level. PUSD's new vision is "Every child will graduate college-ready." Who could argue with this vision? However, something new or different will always stir opposition. As we shared this vision with an educator in another district, the educator looked at us and said, "I don't like that vision. I believe that every child should graduate with the maximum number of options." We were dumbfounded. If students graduate college-ready, how would their options not be maximized?

There will always be resistance to high expectations. Resistance is expected. Only when you overcome that resistance and reach a higher level of success will morale and workplace excellence improve. Although some consider it a cliché, we still value the words in this phrase: "Shoot for the moon. If you miss, at least you will land on a star." People do not feel good about setting mediocre goals and expectations. They feel exactly that, mediocre, when they achieve a mediocre goal.

> "Unless a man undertakes more than he possibly can do, he will never do all that he can."
>
> **HENRY DRUMMOND**

Strategy 4. Create a PLV (Personal Leadership Vision)

If you want your team members to follow your lead, you've got to be absolutely clear about who you are and what you will or will not stand for. A Personal Leadership Vision is extremely important. This vision, which has nothing to do with your department's or organization's vision, is a clear mental picture of how you want others to see you as a leader. Here is an example:

> *I am a leader who truly values the contributions of my people and cares about them as individuals. I am also an enthusiastic leader who has the reputation for taking responsibility, getting things done, and taking calculated risks when necessary. I enjoy the work I do and create an environment in which people have fun!*

The following four suggestions will help you create a Personal Leadership Vision:
- Focus on what you would like your followers to say about you as a leader.
- Write down what you want, not what you do not want.
- Make daily decisions and take actions that support the vision.
- Do not share your vision until you have "walked your talk" for one year.

Developing a Personal Leadership Vision can be a daunting task, so use this technique to make the process easier: Imagine you are being

> **If you want your team members to follow your lead, you've got to be absolutely clear about who you are and what you will or will not stand for.**

honored at your retirement party. Gathered to pay tribute are more than one hundred people who were your bosses, peers, staff people, and customers. Several guests approach the podium to say a few words about the type of manager and person you have been throughout the years. Assume you had an illustrious career.

What would you like your bosses to say about you? How about your peers, staff members, and customers? What qualities do you hope they would mention? What important contributions will you have made to the organization and to the individual lives of your coworkers?

Now, create your PLV. The best Personal Leadership Visions are concise, easy to remember, and evoke passion and commitment.

> "People are more inclined to be drawn in if their leader has a compelling vision. Great leaders help people get in touch with their own aspirations and then will help them forge those aspirations into a personal vision."
> JOHN KOTTER

Strategy 5. Set goals to turn your vision into reality

Here is a simple way to think about goals: Goals are the "I think I cans" of life. When you combine "I think I can" with "I did it," you gain mastery over your life. Abraham Maslow (*Motivation and Personality*) said, "No matter how old you are, the day you cannot sit down and come up with a want list, you are in trouble; you are on the way out."

In working with thousands of supervisors in diverse settings, we noticed that great leaders always have a set of clearly defined goals. We also noted the reverse. Supervisors who struggle in relationships with employees and have difficulty getting their team motivated often express only one ambition: "Just let me survive one more day!"

The accomplishment of anything momentous begins with clear goals. Most people would agree with this statement, yet they lack goals in both their personal and professional lives. Some studies have found that up to 90% of the population does not set goals. Without objectives, you spend the majority of your time reacting to—instead of creating—your environment.

> **Without objectives, you spend the majority of your time reacting to—instead of creating—your environment.**

If you can conceive and believe in your goals, and then take the necessary actions, you can achieve them. It is important to realize that achieving any goal takes persistence, commitment, and a willingness to forego temporary pleasures. Yoda in *Star Wars* was right. When Luke Skywalker says, "All right, I'll give it a try," Yoda responds, "No. Try not. Do or do not. There is no try." That is why in a marriage ceremony when the official asks if you take your spouse for better or for worse, for richer, for poorer, in sickness and in health, to love and to cherish, from this day forward until death do you part, the appropriate response is, "I do"—not, "I'll try."

Goals can be powerful motivators. Goals give you a well-defined purpose, a sense of accomplishment, and a feeling of mastery over your environment. As you set goals, ensure they meet the SMART test: Specific, Measurable, Attainable, Relevant, and Time-bound. Whether you choose to be a committed goal setter or a ship floundering at sea, you must realize one thing: whatever you do with your life, you write your own ticket.

> "The tragedy of life doesn't lie in not reaching your goal. The tragedy lies in having no goal to reach."
> **BENJAMIN E. MAYS**

Strategy 6. **Create a sense of urgency**

Andy Grove, founder of Intel, told an interviewer at *Fast Company* magazine: "When products and services are indistinguishable from each other, all there is by way of competitive advantage is time." In today's business world, speed has tremendous value. Unfortunately, some leaders feel that by changing things slowly, people will not be upset.

Years ago, transitioning word processing from WordPerfect to MSWord was a big deal. One organization announced that it was converting from WordPerfect to Word in six months. Angry employees said, "Fine, but I am not going to convert. I am a WordPerfect user."

Three months before the conversion, the organization started to train the staff on Word. Resisters said, "That's nice to know but I do not need to attend the training because I am not giving up WordPerfect." A month before the conversion, designated trainers from the information technology and human resources departments went out and corralled the few deviant employees into the last training session. At the six-month mark, the conversion took place and the staff had moved through the four stages of change—denial, anger, partial trial, and acceptance.

Another organization practiced fast change. On a Friday night, the leaders, who did not notify employees, deleted everyone's WordPerfect and aligned employees' files with Word. On Monday morning there were many upset people running around saying, "That's okay, I'll find my WordPerfect in the electronic recycle bin." Others were agitated. "How could anyone be so stupid as to take old software off our computers without training us on how to use the new software?"

By 11:00 AM, others were saying that Word was virtually the same as WordPerfect, except for bullets, paragraph indentions, and pagination. By 4:00 PM some people were saying they loved the new software and couldn't believe it took so long for the change.

For the first organization, time (six months) was wasted in implementing the conversion. The second organization took only one day to move people through the cycle of change.

When it comes to the speed of change, how much time does your organization have?

> "People don't resist change. They resist being changed!"
> **PETER SENGE**

Strategy 7. **Align structure for the best interests of the organization**

Is your organizational structure designed in your organization's best interest to achieve the vision? Or has your organizational structure been planned around personalities? When organizations arrange their organizational structure around employees who like each other and/or who refuse to work for certain people, it makes it harder to achieve the vision and difficult to create workplace excellence.

Recently, one organization we work with acquired a competitor. The acquiring organization arranged a new organizational structure and informed the purchased company. Several major leaders in the acquired company told the buyer they would quit if they had to report to the "new" CEO. By accepting its role of "hostage," the acquiring company allowed the leaders to report to the people they liked. Obviously this approach spelled disaster and a year later we were hired to help this organization better understand why making changes was hard, why there was little teamwork at the executive level, and why morale was so low.

When organizational structures are based on personalities, it shields employees from changing their routines or delivering better results. To help bring the organizational structure into alignment, ask yourself this question: If we were to leave personalities out of the decision and design an organizational structure that made the most sense in helping to achieve the organization's vision, what would be the optimal functional organizational structure? The answer will lead you to a better outcome.

But, for those who insist upon structures designed around

personalities, we're grateful. They create more consulting projects for us!

> "I used to think that running an organization was equivalent to conducting a symphony orchestra. But I don't think that's quite it; it's more like jazz. There is more improvisation."
> **WARREN BENNIS**

KEY # 2: COMMUNICATION—THE RIGHT STUFF AT THE RIGHT TIME

Communication is a powerful strategy. When a company encourages employees to express opinions and managers relay the organization's perspective, a team is formed that immediately works to realize the organization's vision. According to 87% of employees in our surveys, leaders in the Best-of-the-Best Benchmark keep employees informed about the company's plans. They even communicate bad news. And, because they give serious consideration to their staff's input, the Best-of-the-Best leaders are in that elite category of two-way communicators.

Strategy 8. **Tell the truth**

On February 9, 2001, Navy Commander Scott Wattles gave an order to perform an emergency maneuver to rapidly surface the 9,000-ton nuclear attack submarine *Greenville*. In a span of eight minutes, Commander Wattles's life forever changed. Nine miles off Oahu, the *Greenville* ripped through the surface of the water and smashed the hull of the *Ehime Maru*, a Japanese fishing boat. The *Ehime Maru* sank within minutes and nine Japanese fishermen died in this tragic accident. To make matters worse, Commander Wattles had been entertaining civilian guests on the submarine and two were at the controls at the moment of impact.

In Commander Wattles's book, *The Right Thing*, he describes his attorney Charles Dickens telling him, "I'll kill you before I allow you to take the stand and testify without immunity. On second thought, I won't have to do it. You'll be killing yourself!"

Wattles knew his attorney was trying to protect him, but he felt compelled to take the stand and tell the truth about what happened. Wattles told his attorney, "There's a time to be silent and a time to speak up for what is right. I'm not the only guy who really knows what happened aboard that ship that day. I'm the only one who knows what I saw through the periscope. I have to tell the truth; I have to take responsibility and let the chips fall where they might. It's the right thing to do."

Wattles was devastated that nine people were dead. He said, "If I was going down, I wanted the truth to be known. Beyond that, my crew was my family. I didn't want anyone else to go down with me." Honesty, when it costs you significantly, is a powerful principle in great leadership. On Friday, December 13, 2002, Scott Wattles made a trip to Japan to offer his personal apologies to the family members of the victims of the accident between the *Ehime Maru* and the *Greenville*. To the Japanese, Scott's apology was a gesture of integrity, humility, and honor.

Establishing a workplace environment of honesty and integrity is extremely important to the future of your business. Being honest and upfront with your employees and management team about their performance is essential for progress and success. If you are a leader respected by both employees and customers, you will receive the benefit of solid relationships and your organization will experience the reward on the balance sheet.

"If you tell the truth you don't have to remember anything."
MARK TWAIN

Strategy 9. Communicate vision and goals to everyone—and do it often

Once your vision is set it will be critical to your success to communicate the vision many times in many ways. In a survey conducted by

Right Management Consultants, two-thirds of employees did not understand their employer's business strategy and were not passionate about their jobs.

The noteworthy reason for this lack of clarity was that 28% of the companies surveyed only communicated this information to their leadership teams; 24% had not yet communicated this information to employees; and 15% were not sure about the best method to communicate this information. The lack of communication resulted in lower employee buy-in, lower productivity, and lower product quality.

Richard M. Kovacevich, former CEO of Wells Fargo, is a great example of a leader who preached a vision over and over. In 1999, Wells Fargo had four financial products in its customers' households. Kovacevich believed that the average consumer purchased fifteen financial products. His vision was to obtain half of the products for Wells Fargo, with a goal of eight Wells Fargo products in each customer's household.

To spread this message, Kovacevich placed updates on the goal in annual reports, Wall Street publications, and in all employee communications. By November of 2008, John Stompf, the new CEO of Wells Fargo reported *a record 5.64 products* per household (*Smart Money*, November 2008). Wells Fargo employees are aware of and focused on the vision. Wall Street analysts pay attention to the vision. Even stockholders are clear on the vision. Wells Fargo is striving to earn more profits from their customers and steal business from competitors. While many financial institutions are excited when they cross-sell one product to a customer, Wells Fargo has a bigger vision. And all the key players are clear about the goal.

> "The very essence of leadership is that you have a vision. It's got to be a vision you articulate clearly and forcefully on every occasion. You can't blow an uncertain trumpet."
> **THEODORE HESBURGH**

Strategy 10. **Create and communicate crystal clear roles and responsibilities**

When roles and responsibilities are muddy, accountability is impossible. Some people actually prefer to work in organizations where roles and responsibilities are blurred because they always have an excuse and someone to blame for poor performance.

Some managers instigate chaos by asking many people to do the same task. Other managers ask employees to do tasks that are traditionally associated with other areas in the organization. This generates confusion and makes it easy for employees to dodge accountability.

Top performers do not like working for organizations where they are not clear on what is expected from them. That helps explain why 85% of the employees at Best-of-the-Best organizations feel their responsibilities are clearly defined, and an outstanding 93% say they understand the organization's performance standards and measurements.

When employees are not clear on their role in accomplishing the organization's goals and what they are responsible for achieving, you may as well blindfold them, spin them around ten times, and tell them to go hit the target. When your organization's vision, goals, and roles are clear, knowing your purpose and the results you are responsible for producing is easy.

 "Good men prefer to be accountable."
MICHAEL EDWARDS

Strategy 11. **Lead with an open-mind policy**

Most leaders say they have an open-door policy. But employees find out quickly that although the door is open, the mind is closed. One employee we interviewed summed up his boss's open-door policy by saying, "My boss's mind is a lot like concrete—thoroughly mixed and set like stone."

If you have an open-door policy, it means you welcome people to your office with their ideas, comments, complaints, and suggestions.

It also means that you actively listen to and honestly respond to those who come to see you. Here are a few tips:

- When people come into your office, invite them to sit down.
- Listen carefully and attentively. Someone came to you, not vice versa. Let the employee talk.
- Ask open-ended questions to seek understanding before you advise.
- Ask the person if there is any action you need to take.
- When people bring you information, thank them. Especially when the information is hard to handle—something you do not want to hear or a problem that you do not want to deal with—thank them.
- Follow-up and take action. If you fail to take action and communicate those actions, people will think, "Why bother?"
- Make it your goal to have a solid understanding of your organization and ask yourself: "Are the right people coming to me so I have a complete picture from different perspectives?"

> "Of all the skills of leadership, listening is the most valuable—and one of the least understood. Most captains of industry listen only sometimes, and they remain ordinary leaders. But a few, the great ones, never stop listening. That's how they get word before anyone else of unseen problems and opportunities."
> **PETER NULTY**

Strategy 12. Ask instead of tell

After more than twenty years of coaching managers and executives, we identified a pattern with leaders who struggle to build relationships. They don't ask, they tell. Sometimes they find it difficult to build a relationship with a boss, peers, or direct reports.

We interviewed a county sheriff who said that his captain yelled at deputies for wasting gas by leaving their squad cars running in the station yard. The captain barked, "I don't care what the reason is, turn your cars off when you are at the station." This deputy went on to add, "You'd think he would ask why we leave the cars running. If he had asked, we would have been able to tell our captain that it takes four minutes to get the on-board computer up and online when we start the car." Four minutes is valuable time when you are being dispatched from the station on an emergency call.

We joke about leaders like this sheriff by saying, "You can try to tell him, but you can't tell him much. Don't try." There are two reasons why we are called to work with struggling managers. First, they are the best "tellers" in the organization. They tell everyone what to do. Second, when they are wrong or there is a better way to do things, they do not like to listen to feedback.

In organizations, executives run to the president to let him know this individual—the teller—is not a team player and is very difficult to communicate with. The direct reports and peers run to human resources to ask for help. Eventually someone says, "The manager needs a coach."

A vice president of human resources forwarded us this e-mail, which includes the original typos, that a manager sent to his team. We could not make this one up.

To: All Staff

Subject: Changes are Coming!

My patience has officially run out! There are some changes coming to our office. If you have not figured it out, I will hold you accountable. In fact if I have to rebuild this market from scratch I will. The first wave of misfits have been removed. A second wave is coming. If you doubt I have the authority you are sadly mistaken. I came here to hold each of you accountable for your activity and to get this market to perform as expected. Since being here I have uncovered a lot of dirt, lack of activity, and the wrong activities, which is sad based on the opportunity and future you could have here. Ever area (position) of the business is under a microscope.

Quite frankly I am tired of not receiving reports on time, or not receiving them at all, failure to follow simple directions and or request, lack of tracking in areas of the business that MUST be tracked. I am tired of folks not taking personal responsibility for success or failures in their area of the business. I have had dealers with out inventory and sales people missing inventory. I have sales people not answering phone calls, or answering the calls two hours to a day late. We have favoritism running rampant in the office, people over reaching on their authority and we have clicks and too much gossip. I see people taking extended lunches and others not clocking out for lunch when taken. I see poor time management. I see an unwillingness to hold outside relationships accountable. I see a lack of urgency when urgency is required.

I can accept nothing less than having the right people on the bus.

As a manager I must inspect what I expect. I don't like what I am uncovering.

Changes are coming!

The only thing this manager did not tell the staff was, "Firings will continue until morale improves."

When the memo writer was questioned about his style of communication, he told the VP of human resources, "Hey, people may not like my style of communication, but I am paid to do a job. And I am just doing my job." We are all paid to do a job. But how we achieve results is also important. This manager was fired shortly after he wrote the memo.

If you want to lead successfully, ask questions. Ask people for their opinions and how you can help them accomplish their goals. When things go wrong, invite their suggestions as well as their commitment to solve the problems. Although the fix is a simple one, our experience is that only about half of the managers we work with are able to do it. The other half tell you why they are the way they are and how the rest of the world is messed up and does not understand why they do the things they do.

"To promote cooperation, remember: people tend to resist what is forced upon them. People tend to support that which they help to create.

VINCE PFAFF

Strategy 13. **Know reality with MBWA (Management by Walking Around)**

The higher you rise in your organization, the greater are the chances of being out of touch with front-line employees and customers.

Today, more and more managers are hiding behind paperwork and are stuck in meetings. This lack of contact with the people who are doing the work causes cracks in communication. Reducing the number of meetings and getting out of your office to talk with employees provides the following opportunities because you can:

- Learn what projects people are working on
- Catch people doing great work and present them with praise and recognition
- Offer coaching when people are not on track or need support
- Keep in touch with the changing realities of departments and the organization

Employees may not respond or may communicate very cautiously at first. But over time you will be able to understand and respond to their concerns and needs. In one employee opinion survey we conducted, mid-level managers scored nearly 30% lower than the executive team on favorable responses to the statement, "Our company has a good understanding of our customers' needs."

When executives saw the discrepancy, several started to chime in on why middle managers thought differently than the executives. A few implied that the managers might not share the same perspective that the executives had about their customers. One executive asked, "More than 250 mid-level managers contributed feedback on this survey and only twelve executives. Is it possible that 250 people may have a clearer picture of reality than we do?"

Another executive said, "We need to get out of the ivory tower and speak to managers one-on-one, beginning the conversation with, 'Middle managers see something that executives are missing when it comes to the needs of our customers. We think you have insight and would like to learn more from you about understanding our customers' needs and improving our products and services.'"

MBWA works well for leaders who are engaged in the daily activities of the business and are committed to spending a percentage of their time every day on the floor and in their offices with employees.

To be effective this approach must be compatible with your management style. It cannot be artificial and you must be committed to use what you learn. Employees will see through you if you are just doing this to check it off your to-do list.

Walk through the building looking for opportunities to give positive comments and receive input and feedback. The more you get out of your office, speak to people, and listen intently, the more accurate your perspective will be. If you think you already know the answers, people will be reluctant to tell you the truth.

> "In organizations, real power and energy is generated through relation-ships. The patterns of relationships and the capacities to form them are more important than tasks, functions, roles, and positions."
> **MARGARET WHEATLY**

Strategy 14. Eliminate the communication lag time

One way to achieve workplace excellence is to remove lag time from your communication, especially the time between making a decision and the time it takes you to inform the people it will affect.

Between 1964 and 1969 there was a classic sitcom on television called *Gomer Pyle, USMC.* Gomer Pyle, played by Jim Nabors, was a bumbling recruit who was always getting into trouble and could never please his drill instructor, Sergeant Carter. Gomer had some priceless expressions that we still remember. One that made Jim Nabors famous was "Shazam, shazam." Another was "Goooolly." Our favorite was "Surprise, surprise, surprise!" In one episode, Gomer said to Sergeant Carter, with excitement, "Surprise, surprise, surprise, we have both been dating the same gal!"

None of Gomer's surprises were good. The same concept applies to surprises in the organizational world. Most surprises to team members are negative, not positive. For example:

■ The project you were working on has been canceled. Surprise, surprise, surprise!

- We have hired someone who you will be reporting to—starting tomorrow. Surprise, surprise, surprise!
- This order needs to be shipped by the end of the week. Surprise, surprise, surprise!
- You made an unnecessary flight because today's meeting was cancelled late last night but we forgot to tell you. Surprise, surprise, surprise!

In an interview about organizational opportunities for improvement, an employee told us that the organization's communication style was NETMA—No One Ever Tells Me Anything.

It's amazing how much information is considered so confidential that it cannot be communicated until the last minute. Of course some things are highly confidential, like ironing out the financial terms of a merger between publicly traded companies. Any information that leaks out could have a devastating effect on the deal. But most things that need to be communicated are not a secret and can be communicated quickly. When you eliminate lag time, employees feel much more valued and are more willing to help you implement the decision.

> "We know communication is a problem, but the company is not going to discuss it with employees."
>
> **SWITCHING SUPERVISOR, AT&T LONG LINES DIVISION**

Strategy 15. Invite HR to the big dance

There is nothing more important to an organization than who gets hired, fired, or promoted. But too often, senior management leaves human resources out of these decisions. Instead of the HR director or VP sitting at the table where the decisions are made, the president or the CFO represents their function. We can often find a senior HR leader taking photos for the company newsletter, planning the holiday party, or being the top cop enforcing a senseless policy.

The HR team can add value and earn the right to sit at the table in the following six areas:

- Recruit and develop the top talent in the industry
- Assist in the design and plan of company business strategies
- Design the organizational structure that accomplishes the strategies and goals
- Recommend the measurements for success
- Resolve conflicts that cause leaders to lose sight of the company's vision and goals
- Assess mergers or acquisitions

If HR leaders want to be contributing members at the big table, they need to:

- Focus on bottom-line results that drive the organization's success
- Quantify the value their department adds to the organization
- Understand and make decisions that support how business works
- Cut red tape that stops people from doing their jobs

When you have an effective human resources leader who understands the business, great things can happen.

> "HR should be every company's 'killer app'."
> JACK WELCH

Strategy 16. In times of crisis, get calmer

Have you ever worked with someone who can take a small problem and blow it out of proportion so that everyone in the organization ends up sharing in the drama? When leaders exaggerate a problem, they telegraph to the entire organization that they do not possess the skills to deal with a major issue.

In the 1970s, I (Peter) earned my way through college by driving an ambulance. On one occasion I was called to an automobile accident that had two fatalities and multiple victims. Six months of emergency training had not totally prepared me for this. I ran back and forth between the victims and the ambulance, yelling at people who were

> **The greatness of a leader is in direct proportion to the size of the crisis that can be handled.**

trying to help. I was in over my head and I knew it.

At the end of the call, I asked my partner, Big Louie, why no one was listening to me at the scene and why everyone was taking direction from him. Big Louie gave me a wake-up call: "Because I can cut it. When you are more nervous and rattled than the victims and people at the scene, you don't give people confidence you can help. Instead, you make the scene worse than before we arrived."

The worse the scene, the calmer you need to be. In times of crisis, great leaders get calmer. They recognize they have been called to lead the organization. People do not follow leaders who lack confidence to lead the organization out of crisis. The greatness of a leader is in direct proportion to the size of the crisis that can be handled.

> "You gain strength, courage, and confidence by every experience in which you really stop to look fear in the face. You must do the thing you think you cannot do."
>
> **ELEANOR ROOSEVELT**

Strategy 17. Focus on what's important

The most significant event in my (Peter's) life was in 1998 when my fourteen-year-old daughter, Brittany, passed away waiting for a heart transplant. For two years during the time she was ill, I lived day to day. Some days were perfectly normal. Other days, Brittany's heart would not properly function, her implanted defibrillator would go off, and my life, along with the things on my to-do list, came to a screeching halt.

Once I had to call a client to cancel a keynote engagement because Life Flight had taken Brittany to the hospital. The client's only response was, "Based on your references when I hired you, I thought we could depend on you." I was devastated. Later that day, when I talked with my friend, Kevin Freiberg, (coauthor with Jackie Freiberg of *Boom!*, *Nuts!*, *and Guts!*) Kevin put it into perspective by telling me, "If she cannot understand what you are going through, that's not your client." Two years later, the same woman was at another organization and she asked me to work with her. The decision to say no to the request was an easy one.

A client who did understand when I called him to reschedule was Betteravia Farms, one of the largest produce growers in California. Joe Prandini, general manager and co-owner, called me and said, "We talked about Brittany's situation this morning in the owner's meeting. If you get a call that an organ is available, we can have our plane in the air within thirty minutes to get you anywhere you need to go. Please call us if we can help."

Major challenges are your opportunity to live your values. For example, when women take maternity leave in our organization, we have only one goal: to keep all the systems in place so the new mom can take all the time she wants to bond with her child.

Is it easy? No. Every time someone on our team takes time off we are nervous that our business needs will not be met. It's critical to ensure that our clients will experience no difference in the service they expect. But the long-term result of doing the right thing is a highly dedicated and engaged workforce who will go to the wall to help get things done.

Whatever your organizational style, you can focus on the right thing at the right time. My wife, Kathleen, has a great saying: "When you are born, that is really big stuff. When you die, that is also really big stuff. Everything else is little stuff." As a leader, your success is dependent on your ability to put things into perspective and focus on what's important.

"The least of things with a meaning is worth more in life than the greatest of things without it."
CARL GUSTAV JUNG

Strategy 18. Promise problems while promising solutions

One of the all-time great examples of promising problems was the Y2K disaster. We were all expecting to wake up on January 1, 2000, and find that computers and technology no longer functioned.

From the 1960s to the 1980s there was a widespread practice in computer software of using two, rather than four, digits for representing a year. This was done to save computer disk and memory space because these resources were relatively expensive in those days. As the '90s approached, experts began to realize this major shortcoming in the computer software applications. Everyone feared that in the year 2000 the computer systems would interpret "00" as 1900, and send us all technologically backward by 100 years. Consequently, a major scare was initiated in almost every industry.

Nicknamed the Y2K bug, the two-digit year was a called a "clicking time bomb" for all major computer applications. For almost two years, IT personnel could not accomplish their technology goals because they "had to put 100% of their resources in the Y2K problem." Most software and application companies came out with Y2K-compliant operating systems to solve the four-digit date problem. Companies around the world spent billions of dollars to go through their entire application source code to look for the Y2K bug and fix it.

Finally, the big day arrived—and nothing horrific occurred. Banks moved money, the IRS collected taxes, and planes flew. (I, Peter, was so concerned that I stayed up past midnight just to check my firm's financial data.) Everything was fine. People had promised so many problems that when none occurred, some people were disappointed.

Promising problems is a safe strategy for leaders because rarely does a significant initiative go exactly as planned. When you only sell the positives of your plan, and complications arise, employees have a tendency to say, "I told you so."

Instead, you should say something like, "We have a great plan but I know there are potentially serious problems to correct along the way. What I am most excited about when I think about these potential problems is that we have a team of experts assigned to this project. If anyone can fix big problems, the people on this team can."

> "Success is never final. Failure is never fatal. Courage is what counts."
> **WINSTON CHURCHILL**

KEY # 3: SELECT THE RIGHT PEOPLE FOR THE RIGHT JOB

The Best-of-the-Best organizations received an outstanding 80% agreement from their employees that the company hired the most qualified candidates for jobs. Not only are the best people hired and promoted, they are also well trained so they can perform at the same level as other high-achieving employees. An employer of choice has the ability to recruit and retain high performers. And much of an employee's satisfaction depends on the actions of his or her supervisor.

Strategy 19. Hire the best people you can find

Kevin and Jackie Freiberg printed T-shirts that read, "HIRE PEOPLE WHO DON'T SUCK." And while we don't intend to, we have all hired such people.

Such people bring a bad attitude, complete assignments late, do not care about the quality of their work, lack accountability, and, if that is not enough, tell everyone in the organization you are a lousy leader. When they walk out the door for the last time, their absence actually brightens up the office.

Southwest Airlines' former CEO Herb Kelleher said, "We hire for attitude and then teach the skill." If you have ever flown on a Southwest flight, you recognize that Kelleher knows the importance of the right attitude. Employees can usually improve upon their skills, but attitudes are harder to change.

Recently, both of us were on a Southwest flight from San Diego to Phoenix. After take-off, the pilot said over the intercom, "We are happy you have chosen to fly with us on Southwest Airlines today. To make your flight as enjoyable as possible, we have a fine crew who will serve you. At Southwest, the pilot and first officer go to a large room each morning and hand-select the finest flight attendants in the industry. Unfortunately, this morning the first officer and I overslept and arrived at the selection room a little late. Monica, Robin, and Shawn were the last three attendants available and we had to pick 'em. We hope you will be kind to them and enjoy the flight."

When we landed, the landing was a little bumpy and hard. Shawn, one of the flight attendants, announced over the intercom, "That abrupt landing was not the pilot's fault." Robin, the second flight attendant, came over the intercom and said, "And that abrupt landing was not the first officer's fault." Monica, the third flight attendant, spoke into the intercom and said, "That abrupt landing was the asphalt. Welcome to Phoenix." It was so obvious this crew had fun flying together, which made a rather dull flight to Phoenix in a full cattle car a ton of fun!

> "People are definitely a company's greatest asset. It doesn't make any differ-
> ence whether the product is cars or cosmetics. A company is only as good as
> the people it keeps."
> **MARY KAY ASH**

Strategy 20. Know the needs and goals of your employees

President Lyndon Johnson was adept at building and maintaining personal connections with just about every individual he met in his personal and private life. He was a great communicator who didn't shy away from making connections. He took time to listen to the goals and needs of others. He was brilliant in the art of human relations. And in 1960 he found himself heading to the White House as vice president with John F. Kennedy.

If you want highly motivated employees, recognize their personal and professional needs and goals. Most managers are so focused on telling people what needs to be done that they have little time to get to know their employees. So ask these seven questions to help you understand your employees:

1. Who's the best boss you have ever had?
2. Who's the worst boss you have ever had?
3. Why have you resigned from jobs?
4. What parts of your job lessen your productivity?
5. What specifically do I do that lessens your productivity?
6. What aspects of your job excite, challenge, motivate, or make you feel proud of your accomplishments?
7. What can I do better to help you accomplish your goals?

Although asking these questions takes time, along with a genuine interest in listening to answers, engaged employees are more productive, stay with you longer, and are much more willing to do whatever it takes to make you—as a leader—and your organization successful.

> "The most basic of all human needs is the need to understand and be understood. The best way to understand people is to listen to them."
> **RALPH NICHOLS**

Strategy 21. Ensure each employee has goals that align to the department, division, and organization

One of the significant keys to creating workplace excellence is ensuring that every employee knows what specific goals he or she needs to accomplish to achieve the organization's vision. It has been our experience that employees who are clear on their goals are motivated to successfully achieve them.

There are a variety of reasons to set employee goals. They focus employees on the purpose of the business, which enhances the chances of your organization's long- and short-term success. Goals also provide purpose to your organization's appraisal and/or bonus program.

To be successful, employee objectives must be concrete, attainable, and critical to the growth of your business. They must also be set with employee involvement. As silly as it sounds, many managers determine their budget and set goals for their team by themselves. Setting goals without the involvement of the employee who is responsible for the goal is not good leadership. When you set goals for other people and ram them down their throats, the goals are usually rejected and hurled back in your direction with excuses about why they are not applicable or appropriate in the specific situation.

Employees are often the best source for information about what job-specific goals will contribute to overall increased productivity, responsiveness, or other business goals. Involving employees also eliminates the potential for the resentment that can arise when goals are imposed.

Legendary Penn State football coach Joe Paterno is known to be a hard-nosed leader who sets high goals for his players and accepts nothing short of perfection in the achievement of them. Yet, his ability to give credit to team members who work well together and lead the team to victory explains why so many high school students dream of playing for him some day. Coach Paterno has coached over twenty-five fathers and, subsequently, their sons.

> "Give me a stock clerk with a goal and I'll give you a man who will make
> history. Give me a man with no goals and I'll give you a stock clerk."
> **J. C. PENNEY**

Strategy 22. Support a meaningful work-life balance

Terry Paulson, CSP, CPAE, is an author, motivational speaker, and past president of the National Speakers Association. Terry encourages participants in his programs to write down the "keepers."

"Keepers" to Terry are the things you learn from others that would be valuable if you incorporated them into your life. One of the "keepers" I (Peter) have learned from Terry is to buy tickets. If you do, you almost always take the time off from work or your normal every day routine to use them. Ever since I heard Terry share this I have planned our vacations at least six months in advance by buying tickets.

Make a list of all the places you would like to see in your lifetime. Make another list of all the events like sporting events, concerts, or plays you want to see. The next step is easy—just buy tickets. Go online and in a very short time you can buy your tickets for the entire year. Book the cruise. Plan the road trip. Arrange the flights and reserve the hotel. I like to pay for the trip in advance. The more commitment I make to the trip or event, the better the chances are that nothing will get in the way of taking time off with my family. You can also plan less expensive events in advance like going to a play or making reservations for dinner.

It is important that you support your staff to maintain a balance between their work and their private lives, too. Encourage your team members to "buy tickets" and take the appropriate time off to use them. When team members come back from time off, it is fun to have them do a brief show-and-tell on what they did while they were away.

Workaholics are not doing their organizations or their families a favor. They tend to be bad at delegating tasks and mentoring others to build organizational capacity.

Go buy some tickets!

> "Sometimes it's important to work for that pot of gold. But other times it's essential to take time off and to make sure that your most important decision in the day simply consists of choosing which color to slide down on the rainbow."
> DOUGLAS PAGELS

Strategy 23. Breathe life into your company with new blood

Diversity has long been linked to a team's success. The reasoning behind this conviction is that diverse viewpoints can ultimately lead to better solutions, which, in turn, can lead to greater success. But does this conventional wisdom actually hold true? Researchers at Northwestern University set out to discover if diversity really does improve team success. Their findings, as reported in the April 29,

2005, issue of *Science*, suggest that although diversity is essential, issues such as race, age, gender, socio-economic status, and religion—which are what most of us think of when we hear the word *diversity*—are *not* the most critical factors in building team success.

So what are the critical factors? After comparing successful and unsuccessful teams, the Northwestern researchers reported two very revealing findings:

- Successful teams had a mixture of *experienced people* and *newcomers* to the field.
- Successful teams had a few *seasoned veterans who had never worked together* prior to joining the team.

This second finding is interesting since people who are tested veterans in a field often have a reputation for carrying huge egos, and big egos usually do not work well together. So what makes a team great is bringing together seasoned veterans who have a strong desire to collaborate and learn from other seasoned veterans. Every successful sports team is a carefully crafted mix of veteran as well as rookie players.

Historically, credit unions would never hire someone with banking experience because credit unions market their very existence on "not being like a bank." Banks, in contrast, have spent enormous sums of money challenging the nonprofit status of credit unions. Mike Maslak, the CEO of North Island Credit Union, a large financial institution in San Diego County, knows the competitive value of bringing new blood into the organization. Maslak broke credit union tradition and hired several veteran bankers to help expand North Island's growth in the San Diego County financial markets. The outcome for North Island has been profoundly positive.

A vital lesson here is that simply introducing new blood is not enough; it has to be the *right* new blood. A careful screening process will enable you to find the perfect combination of types to transfuse new life into your business.

"People have a tendency to want to work with their friends—people they've worked with before. That is exactly the wrong thing to do."
LUIS AMARAL, RESEARCHER AT NORTHWESTERN UNIVERSITY

Strategy 24. **Cut the anchors!**

When it comes to making change in organizations, we believe there are three types of people: propellers, rudders, and anchors. Propellers create positive energy that can help you maneuver in the direction of your vision. Rudders hang off the back of the boat. They neither propel you forward nor inhibit your ability to move. Given a little positive energy and clear direction, they will help guide you where you need to go.

And then there are anchors. Twice in my life I (Peter) have owned a boat. One time when I tried to leave, the anchor was stuck in the mud. Three of us went up to the front of the boat and tried in unison to pull the anchor out. Even with the help of the electric winch we were not able to free the anchor. After about twenty minutes, one of my friends said, "Why don't we just cut the anchor?" My response was, "No way! I have sunk so much money into this, there is no way I am going to cut the anchor. If it went down, it has to come up." We even tried turning the boat around and pulling the anchor out with the power of the engines. Finally I conceded and gave the order, "Cut the anchor!" Once the anchor was cut, we were able to move in the desired direction.

If "anchors" in your organization are unwilling to change after you have spent time coaching, counseling, and training them, then cut them loose and share them with a competitor. Instead of spending too much time with an "anchor," you should focus on developing personnel willing to adapt to an ever-changing business climate. Release one or two change resisters and the rest of the team will quickly say, "I can learn and I can change."

> TIP
>
> **Have a difficult employee that needs coaching? We can help. Go to www.peterstark.com, and enter the word ENGAGE in the Tip Box.**

Tact is critical. Terminating anchors before you communicate clear expectations, as well as provide coaching and training, can induce fear in your organization. The problem with fear in organizations is that your best employees, not the anchors, will be the first to leave. If terminating anchors becomes necessary, use carefully planned maneuvers.

> "It's not that some people have willpower and some don't. It's that some people are ready to change and others are not."
>
> JAMES GORDON, MD

Strategy 25. Formally introduce new hires to the company or division

For over twenty-five years, Anthony Robbins' seminars, videos, and audio recordings focused on personal development have helped nearly 50 million people. The Anthony Robbins Companies, located in San Diego, California, employ over 200 people. Each quarter at the all-employee meeting, the senior management team reviews company successes and opportunities, communicates strategic goals, and reviews actions brought about from the employee opinion survey.

At these quarterly meetings, each new employee is introduced so everyone knows who the person is and where he or she will be working in the organization. Many organizations we work with do this first step. What is most impressive happens next. Senior managers tell the new hires that the team works hard to create a place where employees love to work and they strive hard to hire the best employees to work in this environment. Then they add, "When you strive to hire the best, we know you have a choice where you work. We want to hear from you why you chose to work for the Anthony Robbins Companies." Each new employee then shares the reason.

It is obvious that four things had been accomplished. First, all employees were reminded that the company seeks to hire the best. Second, everyone was able to see who had recently joined the team. Third, new hires felt important and valued by being introduced. Last, when all employees heard the reasons new hires had decided to join the company—most of which centered around the opportunity to grow or work for a company that was focused on helping others—the overall spirit of everyone was raised.

If your organization or team does not formally introduce new team members, we encourage you to do so. But don't stop there. Tell your new hires you know they have a choice where they work and you want other team members to hear why they chose your company.

> "People first, then money, then things."
> SUZE ORMAN

Strategy 26. **Pay people a competitive wage for the job they do**

At a large technology company with affiliate offices throughout the United States, an engineer started off the interview by stating, "I feel like I have just been kicked in the privates." When we inquired about what had happened, the engineer responded, "I hate hiring engineers into our company because new people off the street are demanding almost 20% more as a starting salary than our top-performing engineers, who have been with us over ten years, are currently compensated. And, to add insult to injury, we are asking our veteran top-performing engineers to train these new hires who walk in the door making more money. It is not fair, and the joke in the engineering department is that you need to quit, go to work for another company, and re-apply in a year. Then you will be paid what you are worth."

We recommend that organizations do a salary survey once every eighteen months to two years. Communicate the overall results to the employees who are impacted by the survey. If you are not able to confidently explain the objectivity of your survey, then employees tend to utilize Web sites like monster.com and craigslist.com to gain salary data and believe it as the gospel truth.

> "I don't pay good wages because I have a lot of money; I have a lot of money because I pay good wages."
> ROBERT BOSCH

Strategy 27. Show employees where the money goes

Employees see how much their organization charges a client for their products and services. In interviews, we have had employees tell us, "With what this company charges our customers, you know they should pay us more."

Why not open the books and show employees exactly where the money goes? If you charge a client $1,200 for your service, it is easy to show this breakdown:

Income:	$1,200.00
Expenses:	
Salaries and IRA:	$470.00
Rent:	$110.00
Health Insurance:	$50.00
Office Supplies:	$52.00
Outside Labor:	$46.00
Auto Expense:	$30.00
Dues and Subscription:	$13.00
Depreciation:	$25.00
Contributions:	$6.00
Postage:	$12.00
Printing, Marketing:	$32.00
Travel:	$75.00
Telephone:	$16.00
Taxes:	$42.00
Accounting:	$12.00
Miscellaneous:	$36.00
Total Expenses:	$1,027.00
Gross Profit:	$ 173.00
Taxes:	$ 86.50
Net Profit:	$ 86.50

Now, employees still might think that at $86.50 net profit, the company is not sharing enough money. However, it is a much more realistic figure to float in their minds than $1,200 of gross revenue. Show employees where the money goes.

"The eye sees only what the mind is prepared to comprehend."
HENRI BERGSON

KEY # 4: REMEMBER, WE'RE ON THE SAME TEAM

Each person in the organization needs to see the company's vision. Yet it will be very difficult to reach organizational goals if everyone acts on that vision independently. Teamwork means everyone works together. In Best-of-the-Best organizations, 92% of employees firmly state that their companies place a high value on teamwork. This value is put into action because 89.9% of the Best-of-the-Best staff also say their department works well as a team. As a leader, creating an environment of teamwork is one of your most significant contributions.

Strategy 28. Ensure you're loyal to the right team

To create workplace excellence, collaboration and teamwork must be both demanded and rewarded.

In a January 2006 poll conducted by the Center for Creative Leadership, 275 participants were asked if they saw the challenges faced by leaders today as more complex than the ones faced by leaders five years ago. Ninety-three percent of the respondents agreed that the challenges today are more complex. Over 75% of the respondents went on to elaborate that these complex changes dictated that leaders in their organizations work more collaboratively, improve

> To create workplace excellence, collaboration and teamwork must be both demanded and rewarded.

work processes, and participate in more cross-departmental teamwork.

Many senior and middle-level managers get confused when it comes to deciding which team deserves their true loyalty. They attend executive team meetings to discuss things like vision and strategic goals. As some executives and managers discuss these strategic goals with the management team, their spoken or unspoken conversations focus on protecting their true loyalty, which is their own department.

At one strategic planning retreat we led, everyone on the executive team agreed that the information technology department was not meeting the overall technology needs and vision of the organization. It was obvious that new leadership, new team members, or a new organizational structure was needed in the department. The CTO finally spoke up and said, "I don't think I disagree with what the team is saying. But I need you to know, my department will rebel and some team members will probably quit if we make the changes we are discussing here today." While it was fair for the CTO to point out the issues at stake, the job of senior managers is to make decisions that benefit the organization, not to placate individuals.

When executives and/or managers speak poorly about the management teams they work with, they clearly demonstrate a lack of loyalty. Even worse are the managers who say bad things about their bosses. Speaking poorly about peers or about executive meetings is divisive to the organization and demonstrates to everyone that loyalty is both misdirected and biased.

In each of these examples, managers are indirectly saying that they hold a stronger loyalty to their own team. A house divided will not stand. If executives and managers are not on the same page with a common vision and goals, the only people who take advantage and become successful in these situations are the competitors.

"When we are debating an issue, loyalty means giving me your honest opinion, whether you think I'll like it or not. Disagreement, at this stage, stimulates me. But once a decision has been made, the debate ends. From that point on, loyalty means executing the decision as if it was your own."
COLIN POWELL

Strategy 29. **Meet regularly and often**

One of the greatest tricks played on leaders is listening to employees or peers who tell them, "We don't need to meet." The leader, wanting to be liked, honors the wishes of his employees and peers and cancels the meeting. It has been our experience that teams who are in conflict, or cannot come to agreement on goals or come to consensus to resolve problems, prefer not to meet. As a leader, it is important that you do not fall for the "we don't need to meet" trick. When there are problems or conflicts in your team or in your organization, you need to meet more often until the conflicts are resolved.

We are the first to agree that some meetings are a total waste of everyone's time. By some estimates, at least half of a manager's time is spent in some form of meetings. At the most senior level of organizations, leaders may spend up to 85% or 90% of their work time in meetings. And it is not uncommon for managers and employees to describe some or all of the meetings they attend as a complete waste of their time. But it is important to note that meetings are only a waste of time when the wrong people are in attendance or the right people are missing.

As a leader, schedule a regular meeting for your team/organization. Choose how often your team needs to meet and then delegate the responsibility of setting the day and time to someone else on your team to ensure the get-together happens. Productive meetings tend to occur more often, but for shorter periods of time.

The goal of the meeting is to ensure everyone on the team is on the same page and people are heading toward a common goal. Some of the topics that can be discussed at a daily, weekly, or monthly meeting include:

- Reviewing goals accomplished since the last meeting
- Reviewing goal alignment between the organization and your department
- Solving current challenges or opportunities for improvement
- Updating team members on an individual's progress
- Resolving problems and/or conflicts
- Creating goals and plans for the following week/month

- Bringing up new information that will impact the team in the future
- Recognizing team and individual team member success

To ensure that the meeting is a success, the following guidelines will help to make a productive meeting:

- Create an agenda.
- Ensure team members have input into building the agenda.
- Hold team members accountable to staying focused on the agenda topic.
- Start and stop on time.
- Reward team members who are prepared.
- Coach and counsel team members who are not prepared or do not participate.
- Follow-up by putting the action items into meeting notes and e-mail to all participants.
- Follow-up on action items so team members are prepared for the next meeting.

Don't get tricked. Meet often and be recognized as a leader who leads successful, highly productive meetings.

> "If I am to speak ten minutes, I need a week for preparation; if fifteen minutes, three days; if half an hour, two days; if an hour, I am ready now."
> WOODROW WILSON

Strategy 30. Let the crawdads out

In conducting interviews with government employees in one federal agency, we quickly realized that their morale and spirit may be the worst of any team we have ever partnered with in our combined thirty years of consulting. Interestingly, over 80% of the leaders in this division are eligible for retirement within the next five years. In reality, some had already mentally retired from their job years ago and were anxiously waiting for a formal date of physical separation.

In the middle of an interview, one participant said, "Here is the best way to describe our division: we are just like a bucket full of crawdads." Unfamiliar with the analogy, we asked him to explain. He went on, "I am from Louisiana. When you go crawdad fishing, there is an old saying, 'You don't need a lid for a bucket of crawdads,' because as soon as one crawdad rises to the top of the bucket, another crawdad grabs him and pulls him back into the bucket. That is the way we work around here. If one person gets excited about a change or something new, the rest of us grab her and drag her back down into the reality of working with the federal government, where nothing will ever change."

Every organization has crawdads. Although crawdads make good eating when you visit Louisiana, they are not good team members. Crawdads—team members who suck the life out of others and destroy the team morale and spirit—need to (1) change their attitudes or (2) leave the team. As a leader, it is your job to ensure that one of these two actions materializes in a short period of time.

> "I cannot say whether things will get better if we change; what I can say is they must change if they are to get better."
>
> GEORG C. LICHTENBERG

Strategy 31. Aim ... don't blame

To encourage creative problem solving, it is important to resist the temptation to assign blame when a problem is identified. Blaming others poisons the atmosphere; people defend their actions, which, in turn, limits their creativity as well as their risk-taking efforts when attempting to solve the problem. Any time an organization or department concentrates on "the blame," people focus on covering their assets. Uncovering and resolving problems always takes longer. Organizations and managers who undermine workplace excellence by assigning blame ask these two questions: "What went wrong?" and "Who is to blame?"

It is much more productive to focus the conversation on the future by asking the following two questions: "Where do we want to be?" and "How do we get there?" Engaged employees will respond by asking a third question: "How can I help?"

If you have ever been in a meeting that turned into a gripe session about something or someone, then you know what a blaming discussion sounds like. When discussions focus on who is at fault, nothing is accomplished. As long as someone or something can be blamed, no one needs to be personally accountable until that someone or something being talked about is "fixed."

We recommend letting the blame discussion go on for about three to five minutes and then asking this question: "If we keep this discussion going in this direction, what will we accomplish?" Almost always, a team member will say, "Nothing."

Placing 100% of your energy and focus on where you want to end up, and building a plan to get there, is a key to taking the necessary responsibility to make things happen. Playing a part in the blame game wastes your time, decreases productivity, and has the potential to cause negative financial impacts as a result of productivity decreases. We consider the blame game akin to rolling a snowball down a steep hill and observing the boulder-sized result that is produced toward the bottom of the hill.

> "All blame is a waste of time. No matter how much fault you find with another, and regardless of how much you blame him, it will not change you. The only thing blame does is to keep the focus off you when you are looking for external reasons to explain your unhappiness or frustration. You may succeed in making another feel guilty about something by blaming him, but you won't succeed in changing whatever it is about you that is making you unhappy."
>
> **WAYNE DYER**

Strategy 32. **Value diversity**

Most times when you hear the word *diversity* people are referring to race, gender, age, or religion. Yet we have seen people of the same race, gender, age, and religion with zero tolerance for how others go about conducting business. We also include social or behavioral style under the diversity umbrella.

In our own consulting office several years ago, one employee came into my (Peter's) office and wanted to fire our newest team member because of that person's strong need to ask a lot of questions and focus on the process of how and why we do things. The person who was asking me to terminate this employee was fast-paced and results-oriented and didn't feel a need for questions or process. One of the big reasons we hired the new employee was her style of conducting business; it was so different from that of everyone else on the team. To slow us down, ask questions, and deliver a perfect product or project was exactly what our team needed. About six months later the high-flyer came into my office to tell me she felt that our newest employee helped make a great team.

We believe that by truly valuing diversity, you demonstrate actions that show respect and appreciation for peoples' differences. 3M is one of the best corporations for clearly articulating the value they place on diversity. Their motto is, "Diversity inside = more opportunity outside."

For many people, diversity is about doing the legally right thing. (Most organizations want to avoid being sued.) But organizations that truly value variety as a competitive weapon operate at a level that is even higher than valuing diversity to remain in legal compliance. A workplace that demonstrates an active interest in workers as people first, then employees, can attract and retain a superior workforce.

> "When two men in business always agree, one of them is unnecessary."
> **WILLIAM WRIGLEY JR.**

Strategy 33. **Have a sense of humor**

To be a great team player, it helps to have a sense of humor. Humor facilitates communication and builds relationships in the workplace. In over twenty years of providing executive coaching services, we estimate that less than 10% of executives who are fired lose their jobs because of technical incompetence. The other 90% are let go for their inability to either build a cohesive team or get along with others.

Humor and laughter help to relieve stress in organizations. In fact, it is impossible to feel stress, humor, and laughter all at the same time. Good humor that is supported with jokes, stories, anecdotes, and metaphors helps people to feel good, bond with the person delivering the message, and connect with the organization.

In June 1990, Barbara Bush, wife of former President George H. Bush, was asked to give the commencement speech at Wellesley College. Some students protested the selection of Mrs. Bush as the speaker because they thought that she did not represent the type of independent woman Wellesley sought to graduate. Since Mrs. Bush had only one paying job in the early part of her adult years, the disgruntled students felt that Mrs. Bush's success was a result of her husband's position rather than her own work.

Barbara received an enthusiastic welcome and delighted her audience by concluding her speech with the prediction that someone in the graduating class might someday follow in her footsteps as the president's spouse—"and I wish him well."

Great leaders understand the power of humor and the influence it can have on those they lead. By understanding the opposition to her appearance at Wellesley, Barbara Bush was able to effectively use humor to build a bond with the audience.

"A person without a sense of humor is like a wagon without springs. It's jolted by every pebble on the road."
HENRY WARD BEECHER

Strategy 34. **Just shut up and listen**

On a recent flight to New York, I (Jane) was one of the last two people waiting for luggage at the baggage carousel. For whatever reason, our luggage did not make the flight. I watched as the other passenger became livid, rushed over to the lost baggage counter, and started screaming and swearing at the agent behind the counter. He told the agent, without mincing words, that he intended to sue the airline, the baggage handlers, the pilots, and her for losing his bags. With his final sentence, he nearly spit in her face, "Are you listening to me?" Yolanda, the agent, answered him in a very soft spoken, yet genuine voice, "Sir, the time is 12:14 AM. You need to know that right now, there are only two people in this whole world who care about your lost luggage. It is important for you to understand that with the way you are speaking to me, one of the two is rapidly losing interest."

Accurate information is a vital aspect of listening. But in the business of creating an environment where employees love coming to work, there is a second essential reason to listen. Listening tells others that you care about them and you value their opinions.

You can build an environment where people feel cared about and valued by using these five tips:

- Be motivated to listen. The more you can learn, the better off you will be.
- If you must speak, ask questions. By moving from broad to narrow questions, you will eventually acquire the information you need to make the best decisions.
- Be alert to nonverbal cues. Although it is critical to listen to what your counterpart says, it is equally important to understand the attitudes and motives behind what is being said.
- Let your counterpart speak first.
- Do not interrupt when your counterpart is speaking. Interrupting a speaker is not good business.

> "So when you are listening to somebody, completely, attentively, then you are listening not only to the words, but also to the feeling of what is being conveyed, to the whole of it, not part of it."
> **JIDDU KRISHNAMURTI**

Strategy 35. To see the whole team, get up in the balcony

In 2005 and 2006, Steve Nash, the point guard for the Phoenix Suns, became one of a handful of players in the National Basketball Association to win the coveted Maurice Podoloff Trophy as the NBA's Most Valuable Player two years in a row. What is remarkable is that at six feet, three inches tall, Nash is one of the shortest players in the NBA. Nash joined Hall of Famer Magic Johnson as the only point guard in league history to capture multiple MVP trophies. He became one of only nine players to win the award in consecutive seasons.

When Nash was awarded the 2006 award (fifty years after the inaugural award was given in honor of the first commissioner of the NBA, Maurice Podoloff), Commissioner Stern said, "Steve Nash is a star, but what is most significant is that the four other players on his team all averaged double digit points in every game. He makes other players even better."

What helps Steve Nash lead his team to greatness is his ability to play hard while keeping the whole game situation in mind. When Nash runs down the court or sets up his move for the basket, it is as if he hovers in the balcony above the court. Most players are so intensely involved in their own play they are not aware of who is mismatched with a defender or who is open for a pass. This is what makes Nash so difficult to defend. Just when you think he is going to pass the ball, which he is most accustomed to do, he keeps it and scores.

Business team leaders need to be able to:

- Think tactically and get the job done.
- View the entire organization from a "bigger picture" perspective.
- Honor an organization's history.
- Gain a strong perspective about the changes in the economy, environment, and their industry.

Great leaders need to have the ability to move back and forth between the tactical sides of their job and to set up a more global perspective.

> "What we see depends mainly on what we look for."
> JOHN LUBBOCK

Strategy 36. Honor people's time

One of the best ways you can tell people that you really care about them and value them is to honor their time. We have worked with several executives that are certifiably addicted to their CrackBerrys. We can be sitting in a one-on-one meeting with them and every thirty seconds they pull out their vibrating BlackBerry or Trio to read an e-mail. Worse, they look at us and say, "Just a minute," as they respond to the latest message. This sends out a really strong signal that their time, and the time of the person they are responding to, is more valuable than we are. And if they do it to us, they do it to others.

Recently, a manager I (Peter) was meeting with began reading his e-mail. I said, "Let me guess. It is another opportunity to buy Viagra online." Stunned, he looked at me and said, "No, but it is unimportant. I will respond later." Another amazing example of showing people you don't value their time is the person who does not turn off the cell phone while in a meeting. As if that is not enough of a problem, some people raise arrogance to a whole new level by answering their phones in a meeting or seminar and then talking to the caller while the meeting is in progress.

> One of the best ways you can tell people that you really care about them and value them is to honor their time.

On one Sunday, someone in our church congregation answered his phone and started a conversation during the sermon. Still, that is not as weird as the people who use their cell phones in a public restroom. The other day, some guy in the stall next to me said three times, "Hello. Hello. Hello." When I said, "Hello. How are you?" the next thing I heard was, "Can I call you back? Some idiot in the stall next to me is trying to talk to me."

The following are several suggested ways for you to send the signal to others in your organization that you do honor their time.

- Don't answer your phone when you are meeting with another individual.
- Don't read your e-mail when you are meeting with someone one-on-one or you are in a meeting.
- If you are going to be late for a meeting, call the person you have scheduled the meeting with, apologize, and let that person know you will be late. Offer the opportunity to re-schedule the meeting at another convenient time.
- Be organized so you can give your staff the proper time to work on your projects.
- If the project is not a crisis, ask your staff or peers when they have time to meet with you.
- Thank people for giving you their time.
- When people need help, give them your time, or a time when you are available.
- Copy people on your e-mails or voice mails when you will ultimately need their support to complete the task. When you copy others on e-mails, notify them if you need them to take specific action.

> "Time is at once the most valuable and the most perishable of all our possessions."
> JOHN RANDOLPH

Strategy 37. Go FISH and have fun!

One sarcastic definition of work is, "You'd rather be doing anything else." It's a shame to spend so much time at work and still view its drudgery as normal. Fortunately, the opposite is also true. To love what you do—and have fun doing it—makes a job not seem like

> **Research has shown that employees with a sense of humor are perceived to do a better job because they are less rigid, more flexible, and less stressed out.**

work. Interestingly, research has shown that employees with a sense of humor are perceived to do a better job because they are less rigid, more flexible, and less stressed out. It's definitely something to consider in every job interview.

In addition to finding the right people, it helps to support an environment that is fun. In 2000, Stephen C. Lundin, PhD, Harry Paul, and John Christensen wrote a bestselling book called *FISH!* The book profiled Seattle's Pike Place Fish Market where the workers joke with each other and their customers. Fun is the operative action—the employees even throw fish to each other.

Any workplace can be enjoyable. Having or not having fun at work is a choice that everyone makes. There are a few essential ingredients of an enjoyable atmosphere:

- Fun must be valued and regarded as an important part of the work environment.
- Fun must be a part of your everyday work.
- Fun must be planned. Get your team together and let them create a calendar with "fun" events.
- Think funny! If you love humor, you will constantly be looking for opportunities to express yourself.

Tim Fennell, the general manager of the San Diego County Fair, one of the largest fairs in the United States, knows the importance of having fun. Tim took four hours out of the organization's strategic planning retreat to take the entire management team go-kart racing. The next morning, everyone on the team was talking about how much fun they had competing with each other and cheering for their teammates.

To generate ideas on how to enjoy work time, a great resource is

Dave Hemsath's and Leslie Yerkes's book *301 Ways to Have Fun at Work.*

"The supreme accomplishment is to blur the line between work and play."
ARNOLD TOYNBEE

Strategy 38. Do something significant for your community

People like to get behind a good cause. Helping a community organization imparts a wonderful feeling that MasterCard would describe as "priceless." Whether it is a team running in a 10K or taking a sixty-mile, three-day walk, the time spent together on a cause builds unity and teamwork. It also shows the compassion and heart that is alive in the organization.

One great example of this was when we conducted a two-day retreat with Wells Fargo Mortgage Resources. At the end of the first day, we all boarded a bus and headed to a homeless shelter in the poorest section of downtown San Diego. This shelter's clientele was homeless women with young children. Kathleen Vaughan, senior vice president, and her team of leaders helped get dinner ready, made up the beds for the evening, read books to the children, and did a lot of talking about life with the moms.

Seeing kids without a home is heart-wrenching. This experience was profound for us as consultants and as parents. Kids are incredibly resilient. There was not one child who was sitting on a pity pot because of spending a night in a shelter. These kids were happy, healthy, and overjoyed to have someone read a book or sing songs with them. As consultants we saw that the teamwork, which was good on day one, was significantly enhanced on day two because of the teambuilding experience that had occurred at the homeless shelter the night before. We observed that everyone on the team had a huge heart and felt really good about giving back to the community and being able to make someone else's life better, if only for one night.

"Think of giving not as a duty but as a privilege."
JOHN D. ROCKEFELLER JR.

KEY # 5: COOL STUFF—CONTINUOUS IMPROVEMENT AND INNOVATION

Innovation is one of the top ten most significant differences between the organizations in the Best-of-the-Best Benchmark compared to those in the Overall Benchmark. Best-of-the-Best companies understand that innovation—and the accompanying improved quality, efficient business processes, and competitive position—results from harnessing and rewarding the talents of innovative people. According to 79.5% of the staff, Best-of-the-Best organizations expect innovative ideas, which is a likely reason why these companies are highly competitive. Better yet, 84.5% of employees feel that the Best-of-the-Best recognize the people who come up with innovations. That's a sure way to keep the original ideas—the cool stuff—flowing through the company and out to the customer.

Strategy 39. Great leaders keep people uncomfortable

Yes, great leaders keep their people uncomfortable. The more traditions and long-term employees your organization has, the more pressure employees put on managers not to change things quickly—to keep them comfortable. A favorite line used by employees who work for organizations with a strong history of following traditional methods is, "We are not opposed to change. We just don't like fast change." A second classic is, "Not all change is good change."

Both of these famous lines deserve comment. First, the people who say, "We just don't like fast change" exhibit behaviors that signal they don't like any change. You could tell them six months in advance that their cubicle location was going to change, and they would resent the advance notice about as much as finding out on the same day they had to move. Second, everyone is in agreement that not all change is good change. Traditionalists fail to acknowledge that improvement in organizations never occurs without change.

In one organization we worked with, the information technology department had built a reputation of being nonresponsive to employees' and management needs. The IT team members worked on projects they personally found interesting. And, to ensure they kept their jobs, they defended technologies that were no longer meeting the organization's long-term goals. The vice president knew his department was not meeting the organization's needs, but every time he tried to implement a change, team members rebelled. We should have changed the vice president's title to "hostage."

In another organization, a disgruntled employee approached us at the end of our seminar entitled "Surviving and Thriving Organizational Change" and said, "You have no right to tell our managers that it is their job to keep us uncomfortable." She continued, "Managers in our company have no clue how stressful our jobs already are." The real challenge for this employee was that she was caught between a rock and a hard place. She did not like her job. She was providing poor customer service while customers were raising the bar on the level of service they were demanding from vendors. This story has a short ending. That employee was shared with a competitor.

We are being practical when we say that leaders who keep their people comfortable for longer than three to five years usually end up losing their jobs. This happens because every time they try to make a change, the team members resist because they do not like change. Instead of challenging the employees and holding them accountable to the adaptation, the leader backs off and allows the followers to assume their normal routine. Three to five years later, the department or team is so far out-of-sync with the rest of the world that the only thing to do is fire the leader. This drastic action occurs because the leader does not have the relationship needed to implement even basic change with the employees.

Raise the bar. Hold people accountable. Speed up the pace of change to gain advantage over a competitor. Great leaders keep their people uncomfortable and unsatisfied with complacency.

"Do not let what you cannot do interfere with what you can do."
JOHN WOODEN

TIP

Need help navigating the sea of change?
Go to www.peterstark.com, and enter the word
ENGAGE in the Tip Box.

Strategy 40. Innovate and outperform your competition

In 2006, the Boston Consulting Group analyzed the top twenty-five most innovative companies to see if they had a more profitable bottom line. The research, conducted for *Business Week* magazine using data generated from Standard and Poor's (S&P) Compustat, demonstrated that it pays to be an organization with a reputation for innovation. The innovators achieved a profit margin growth of 3.4% a year since 1995, compared with 0.4% for the median Standard and Poor's Global 1200 company. The innovative companies' median annual stock return was 14.3%, which was 3% higher than the S&P 1200 over the decade (*Business Week*, April 24, 2006).

The key to success is to pair innovative mentors with people who have a high potential to be innovative, and then give these individuals ample opportunities to practice. Employees love to work for organizations that strive to improve by working on cool stuff. 3M began its Carlton Society, which consists of very successful innovators who serve as advisors throughout the company. Proctor and Gamble started Connect + Develop, a program designed to encourage "open innovation." And Apple Computer established its Apple Fellows project teams dedicated to innovation during the company's start-up years. Being committed to innovation and making that commitment clear to all members of an organization led to such accidental innovations as brandy, X-rays, penicillin, Silly Putty, potato chips, and microwave ovens.

One of the best examples of corporate innovation is Netflix, the online mail-order DVD rental company. In 1999, Netflix decided it was more convenient to order DVDs online (with no due dates or late fees) than it was to drive to Blockbuster or Hollywood Video. By 2006, Netflix counted more than seven million subscribers. In a recent seminar with one hundred participants, we asked, "How many of you have gone to Blockbuster or Hollywood Video in the last month?" Eleven people raised their hands. We then asked, "How many subscribe to Netflix or another online service and received a DVD by mail during the last month?" Thirty-seven people raised their hands. Even our eighty-eight-year-old father has 104 DVDs cued in his Netflix account. Netflix's award-winning customer service has allowed the company to outmaneuver Blockbuster and Hollywood Video because of its innovative approach.

Then there is Sony, which was hesitant to release its digital music player until the company could ensure copyrighted music could not be illegally downloaded. Apple, with a very different goal, focused on creating technology to efficiently download, store, and play digital music. The end result: The iPod made history.

The corporate graveyard is full of organizations with a prescription for success but who did not anticipate or produce the next product or service the consumer would need.

Innovate and outperform your competition.

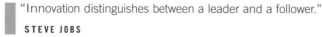

"Innovation distinguishes between a leader and a follower."
STEVE JOBS

Strategy 41. Personally change first

Being a leader in an organization during these turbulent times is challenging and, occasionally, can seem like an overwhelming task. During the past ten years, every organization has felt the impact of change through: rapid growth or downsizing, increased expenses and decreased profits, expanding or crumbling markets, more competition and advanced technological demands.

All are indicators that organizations will continue to face challenges pushed by sharp economic swings, keen competitive pressures, global ization of the marketplace, and reshaping of businesses worldwide. Simply put, change is the reality and the organizations that refuse to acknowledge that reality will not survive what some have called "The Age of Instability."

The most important distinction to remember is that organizations do not change. It is the people who work for these organizations who do so—on an individual basis. And when they do, they empower the organizations to change. Unfortunately, it's a given that not all employees respond to altering the status quo with the attitude of, "Fantastic! Another organizational change and I'm excited to be a part of it!" Strong-willed employees are like dinosaurs. They may be well on the path to extinction, but they will fight each step of the way.

We have found that when change is introduced to an organization or, better yet, rumored, leaders will respond in one of three ways.

First, some of the strongest-willed leaders will fight organizational change, even when deep down they recognize that the change is in the best interests of the organization.

The second type of leader takes a "let's wait and watch" approach. These leaders will not fight an organizational change because they do not think that it will directly impact them. They dig their heels in deeply and hope that the change will eventually pass them by.

Last, the third type of leader is able to accurately assess the future and possesses the flexibility to adapt accordingly. Typically, they are excited about changes and have anticipated the organization's need to do so.

As a leader, you are the role model. The attitude you convey will be contagious. When leaders anticipate the need for change and get excited about role modeling the change, the dinosaurs either change or become extinct.

"The most important thing is this: To be able at any moment to sacrifice what we are for what we could become."
CHARLES DUBOIS

Strategy 42. **Be a role model for leading the new change**

The only change that really exists is personal change. You can't force people to change, but you can lead a change effort and be a role model for it. So, as a leader, what specific actions can you document that you altered over the last year? If the leader does not change, you can tell team members they need to change but, most likely, it is not going to happen. Try following these actions used by leaders who have helped pilot organizational change and improve workplace excellence.

Involve employees in the change process. We are firm believers that employees are not so much against change as they are against *being* changed. It is incredibly important that you, as a leader, fully understand the meaning of the previous statement. The sooner you involve employees in the process the better off you will be at implementing the change.

Ask, don't tell. People who do not deal well with change are generally the same employees who cannot be "told" anything. For this reason, try asking them questions rather than stating why the changes are taking place.

Get both negative and positive informal leaders involved. Most managers and supervisors involve the positive informal leaders in helping implement changes because they have a reputation for supporting management. The mistake is not getting the negative informal leaders involved in the beginning stages of the change process. Since negative informal leaders are usually left out, they lack commitment and may even try to sabotage the change. By involving them, their behaviors will change.

> **Employees are not so much against change as they are against *being* changed.**

Besides, when you know what their objections and concerns are, it will help you design your strategy. Finally, if you can meet their concerns, they will help sell the change to the rest of the organization.

Raise expectations. While it may be more practical to expect less in terms of performance, this is the time to raise performance levels for both yourself and your employees. During change, employees are more likely to modify their work habits. Seize the opportunity and push them to try harder and work smarter. Require performance improvements and make the process challenging, but remember to keep goals realistic so you can eliminate the frustration and failure that accompany an unfulfilled objective.

Ask employees for their commitment. Once the change has been announced, it is important that you personally ask for each employee's commitment to successfully implement the change.

Over-communicate. The change process usually means that normal communication channels in the firm won't work as well as they usually do. During this time, your employees will be hungrier than ever for information and answers. You can "beef up" communication in two ways. First, offer employees an opportunity to give you input. Second, strive to clear up rumors and misinformation that clutter the communication changes. Remember, it is almost impossible to over-communicate.

Stay positive. Your attitude will be a major factor in determining what type of climate your employees feel. Change can be stressful and confusing so try to remain upbeat, positive, and enthusiastic. During times of transition and change, compensate your employees for their extra effort. Write a little note of encouragement and drop it on an employee's desk. Leave a nice message on someone's voicemail. E-mail a word of thanks or encouragement. Take employees aside and tell them what a great job they are doing. Last, try to portray organizational change as a personal challenge.

As football players look to their quarterback for guidance and inspiration on the field, your employees look to you for the same in the game of business. If the quarterback does not instill confidence in his teammates, the team's offense suffers and victory becomes uncertain. With the increasing number of uncertainties that businesses face today, the future promises both challenges and opportunities. As a leader it will be your responsibility to overcome the obstacles and succeed. Will you lead your team to that end-zone in the boardroom and on the balance sheet?

> "A leader takes people where they want to go. A great leader takes people where they don't necessarily want to go, but ought to be."
>
> **ROSALYNN CARTER**

Strategy 43. Encourage and reward employees' ideas, suggestions, and recommendations

Many managers believe that they encourage employees to offer ideas, suggestions, and recommendations to improve the company. Some employees do offer input. Other employees come in each day, do their work, and then leave.

The latter come to work each day and, having done their job for so long, never have to think. Some disgruntled employees have even been quoted as stating, "They don't pay me enough to think." It is difficult to create workplace excellence unless everyone on the team thinks about what needs to be done, specifically what each individual can do, to improve the organization.

The Best-of-the-Best organizations we survey not only encourage employees to provide ideas and suggestions—they expect it. Then, they build this expectation into the performance management system so they can reward the employees who come up with the cool stuff. When employees are rewarded for innovation, they continue to innovate.

Encouragement is a great thing. Outlining expectations, then recognizing and rewarding people for meeting those expectations, is even better.

> "The spirited horse, which will try to win the race of its own accord, will run even faster if encouraged."
>
> OVID

Strategy 44. Change what you reward

Does your organization need to change to be even more competitive in the marketplace? If so, the fastest way is to also change what you reward. When you reward with the exact same thing you have for past years, you are most likely going to get the exact same result.

Some years ago, one of the rites that followed passing the bar exam and becoming an attorney in a large law firm was being rewarded with a personal secretary or paralegal. As law firms consolidated and worked on becoming more productive and profitable, people realized that with computers, it was no longer necessary to maintain a one-to-one attorney/secretary ratio. One secretary or paralegal, with the help of technology, could support two or three attorneys.

If you want to see a war, take away an attorney's personal secretary or paralegal. The secretary, the paralegal, and the attorney will fight to avoid sharing their human resources with another attorney. This was a war that the secretaries were winning until the law firms changed what they rewarded. When the firms developed a bonus system that was based on productivity, change occurred rather quickly. These firms informed the secretaries and paralegals that if they were only able to handle the work of one attorney, they would receive up to a 5% bonus. If they were able to handle the work of two attorneys, they would be eligible for a 10% to 15% bonus. Finally, a secretary or

When you reward with the exact same thing you have for past years, you are most likely going to get the exact same result.

paralegal who was able to handle the work of three or four attorneys would be eligible for a bonus of 15% to 20%.

Another organization we worked with paid a commission on how many physicians were recruited into their HMO network. The challenge to making the sale and earning a commission was that many of the recruiters negotiated outcomes with physicians who were not profitable to the company. When the company started a new hybrid system of paying the recruiters who considered both the sale and the profitability of the sale, behaviors quickly began to change.

When you change what you reward, behaviors will follow. Although it is unfortunate that incentives too often drive human work ethic and boost results, not accepting this fundamental truth can be disastrous for your organization.

> "Start with good people, lay out the rules, communicate with your employees, motivate them, and reward them. If you do all those things effectively, you can't miss."
> LEE IACOCCA

Strategy 45. Honor and cherish the past

Don't put down or speak poorly about the way your team, your organization, or your employees conducted their business in the past. In several executive-coaching sessions, leaders have shared that the very reason their employer hired them was because things were messed up and they were there to fix the problem. These executives may be 100% accurate. Most people do not get hired because everything is perfect. But, when you put down the past you provoke divisive relationships where people quickly lose their motivation to follow you.

Comments like the following do nothing except destroy morale, even if they are true.

- Our technology is antiquated. We need to get in line with the twenty-first century.

- Our processes and/or systems are broken.
- Our people are poor performers because they really believe they cannot be fired.
- Our people do not want to change.
- Because our people have worked so long for this company, they have no clue what goes on in other successful organizations.
- We are totally out of touch with the needs of our customers.

There is another strong reason for not putting down your organization or your department's past. What already happened was good enough to invite you to join the team. A better strategy is to honor the past, and then communicate how your goals and actions can make the future even better. It also helps to admit that you do not have all the answers and ask for the team's help in finding them.

The minute you put down a company's history, there are always some employees thinking this thought: "I was here before you, and I will be here after you leave." Many times, employees with this attitude orchestrate the undermining and removal of the manager who has been brought in to save the organization. How can this be?

If you put down the past, you destroy people's self-esteem and morale. People fight hard to maintain their dignity and self-esteem. Honoring and cherishing what went before, along with a game plan to work toward an even better future, builds teamwork and creates a motivated workforce devoted to helping, not undermining, the new leader.

"You have to know the past to understand the present."
DR. CARL SAGAN

KEY # 6: RECOGNIZE AND REWARD EXCELLENT PERFORMANCE

Equally rewarding mediocre and excellent performances is a sure way to lower motivation and decrease morale. The Best-of-the-Best organizations know this, so they exclusively reward above-and-beyond achievement. Employees are well aware of this distinction; 73.4% of workers in the Best-of-the-Best companies feel that the highest achievers are appropriately rewarded. According to 80.2% of their employees, those top-tier organizations also inform others of the individual's success in order to encourage others to reach for the same levels of excellence.

> **TIP**
>
> Like to know how to give a powerful (yet painless) performance review? Go to www.peterstark.com, and enter the word ENGAGE in the Tip Box.

Strategy 46. Take recognition off your things-to-do-list

We used to tell leaders that they needed to add the recognition of three people to their to-do list each day. We were not picky about who our leaders recognized. It could be their direct reports, their boss, a peer, or even their spouse. As we've learned more about what employees value, we've altered our thinking about recognition.

Cindy Ventrice, author of *Make Their Day! Employee Recognition That Works*, states, "Take recognition off your things-to-do list. Recognition isn't something you can do and then check off your list. You need to think of recognition a little differently. Find ways to add recognition to every employee interaction." What Ventrice is asking all of us to do is to make praise and recognition a part of everything we do in our lives.

Being grateful for individual contributions is an important step in creating engaged employees and workplace excellence. As a leader, recognizing people each day—and genuinely meaning what you say—forms relationships in which more people are willing to follow you and help you achieve the organization's goals.

> "Appreciate everything your associates do for the business. Nothing else can quite substitute for a few well-chosen, well-timed, sincere words of praise. They're absolutely free and worth a fortune."
>
> SAM WALTON

Strategy 47. **Planned, spontaneous recognition works best**

We are big believers in planned, spontaneous recognition. And, we are well aware that spontaneity isn't planned and plans aren't spontaneous! Plan to make recognizing success a daily habit by looking around you at the work being performed. Instead of planning a formal award and announcing it, make your recognition more spontaneous.

In a recent meeting, a vice president stood up and said, "No one knows what I am about to do, but it is always important to recognize great work." He proceeded to call a manager up to the front of the room. The manager was dumbfounded; she had no idea why she was being singled out.

Then the vice president made the following speech: "In our values, we talk about exceeding customer expectations. In our values, we also talk about innovation. Over the last three weeks, I have received three phone calls or e-mails from clients praising the level of support they received from the customer support department. Living that value alone is worthy of recognition. But the reason I called Margaret up today is not only because her department is giving great service on a daily basis. Margaret and two of her team members are actively involved in implementing a new Web site for our customers. I have seen a couple of additions to the Web site and it is incredibly innovative. Some of the things Margaret and her team are working on I have never seen before and I think they are going to give us a significant competitive advantage."

The vice president ended his speech by shaking Margaret's hand and telling her he knew how many extra hours she had been putting into this project. Then he handed her a $200 check to take her family out for a meal on the company in recognition of her meaningful work.

It is important to note that things like bonuses and perks are not recognition. We know one business owner with fifteen employees who pays to have his employees' cars detailed each week. Another department manager buys lunch for her team one day each week. These are fabulous perks, but they are not recognition. Planned, spontaneous recognition works best when:

- What you are praising and why is crystal clear
- Praise or recognition is specific
- Praise is proportional to the accomplishment
- Praise is timely

   You will find that most employees respond well to public acknowledgement of their accomplishments, especially after they have placed a considerable amount of their time into the project. It is critical you understand that by overindulging your entire workforce in benefits/perks that they have not earned or cannot appreciate could produce a deadly complacency that would cripple your productivity. This is precisely why spontaneity is crucial to the provision of recognition, perks, and rewards.

> "Nothing is more effective than sincere, accurate praise, and nothing is more lame than a cookie-cutter compliment."
> **BILL WALSH**

Strategy 48. Appropriately reward the highest achievers

In an interview at a large, publicly traded, market-leading technology company located in San Diego, an engineering manager shared this story. Both the manager's manager, a senior-level vice president, and a human resources manager agreed upon three things. One, the engineering manager was the most technically qualified in his division. Second, based on his starting salary and length of service, he was paid in the lowest quartile of the company's salary scale. And finally, there was little hope of moving him to the top quartile because the company had a moratorium on wage increases.

   The maximum increase a top-performing employee could achieve on this performance review cycle was 2%. When we asked this manager how much he felt he was underpaid, he responded, "Human resources has verified that I am about 30% below market, but there is nothing they can do about it because of this moratorium on wage increases."

This disengaged manager and many other top performers in the organization were dealing with their lack of appropriate compensation by withholding some discretionary effort. They made the conscious decision to do what they had to do to get their job done, but nothing more.

The impact of not appropriately rewarding the highest achievers is that they start to question why they should go out of their way to work hard and produce extraordinary performance when there is no correlation between top performance and remuneration.

As an organization, this is a scary situation. This technology company is relying on successful, extremely technical product launches over the next two years. The people who are directly responsible for these new product introductions are contributing about 50% effort because they do not feel they are either competitively or appropriately compensated.

Evaluating people based on their performance is a wonderful concept. Assigning people to a specific pay scale, based on performance, is also a good idea. However, this organization and the executive committee missed providing the highest rewards to the top performers. When you only do one half of the compensation equation—defining what great performance looks like—but forget about the second half of the equation—compensating people for great performance—it is equivalent to telling people to win the race and when they do, tell them they did win, but give them a fourth place medal. When you do not appropriately reward the maximum achievers, it is nearly impossible to create long-lasting workplace excellence.

Today the strategy of rewarding the highest achievers is being applied even in industries where traditionally everyone has been paid commensurately, regardless of performance, like education. On January 23, 2007, The Houston Independent School District (HISD) took a sizeable risk in the business of education by changing the teacher compensation model and paying a bonus to the teachers who increased student test scores. Abelardo Saavedra, superintendent of the district, stated, "Today is really one of the most important days in HISD history." The HISD school board set aside $14 million this year for bonuses to reward top teachers and lure the top teachers from other school districts. Forty-two teachers received bonuses of $6,000 or more. The average teacher bonus was $1,800. As anyone familiar with the business of education would expect, the teachers unions are adamantly opposed to any pay system that would pay one teacher differently from another. Gayle Fallon, the president of the Houston Federation of Teachers, stated, "I think my members are all great teachers. This is one of the worst things I have seen done for HISD teacher morale." A teacher, Lisa Auerbach, stated, "If you've got the money, then just give it to us in our salaries. We go to work at 7. We come home around 4 or 5. Don't make us jump through hoops." (*Houston Chronicle*; Wednesday, January 24, 2007)

The Best-of-the-Best know that it is critical to reward top performers for their results, even when everyone in the organization is not in agreement.

> "We will receive not what we idly wish for, but what we justly earn. Our rewards will always be in exact proportion to our service."
>
> **EARL NIGHTINGALE**

Strategy 49. Find a reason to celebrate

One of our clients utilizes a clever form of celebration that started with one salesperson's need to bring attention to his first big sale. When the salesperson made a sale worth over $10,000, he stood up in his cubicle and honked a horn that had fallen off his son's bicycle. The next day, another salesperson made a $10,000 sale and he rang a bell from a child's bicycle. When the second salesperson rang his bell, the first salesperson honked his horn to join in with the celebration.

Today, every person on the floor keeps some type of noisemaker and joins the celebration when someone makes a significant sale. One engineer with a warped sense of humor came out of his office to squeeze his whoopee cushion. Even the president and the vice presidents come out of their offices to bang pots and pans or sound a trumpet. What is exciting is that these celebrations are not restricted just to sales. Celebrations also take place when new employees are hired or start their first day at work, major projects are completed, and actual end-of-month results exceed the budget.

We imagine that there are many leaders who are reading this right now and thinking, "Isn't all this noisy celebration disruptive to an environment conducive for business?" For many organizations, this method of celebration would probably be disruptive because they do not place a high value on celebration. At this organization, the people on the team are incredibly supportive of each other and take pride in bringing attention to each other's successes. Here, people look for a reason to sound their noisemakers. Knowing how to celebrate success, they enjoy it.

"Celebrate what you want to see more of."
TOM PETERS

Strategy 50. Honor special days

Everyone is so busy. They don't have time to spend celebrating someone's birthday or a special occasion. There are many people in the world who are only focused on achieving the goal and counting the money that drops to the bottom line. These types of people believe that subtracting time out of the day to recognize a special occasion wastes time, costs too much money, and is not all that necessary anyway.

Nothing could be further from the truth when it comes to creating workplace excellence. The Western Growers Association carves time out of every employee meeting to honor noteworthy employee accomplishments and anniversary milestones. To call someone out of his or her office or cubicle into the conference room to sing and share cake on their special day—whether a birthday or ten-year anniversary with the company—is an easy way to say, "You are really important to us and the organization's leaders support us in taking this quick time out to acknowledge you."

In interviews, we hear this comment over and over: "We used to be like a family around here. We used to celebrate birthdays, but now we don't do that anymore. I guess management doesn't care about our people any longer."

Many years ago, we consulted with American Residential Mortgage Corporation (AmRes), now an acquisition of the Chase Manhattan Corporation. AmRes was the best at honoring employees on their special days. One day, I (Peter) was walking among the cubicles when I noticed one manager's space had a bunch of balloons hung up all around it. I went up to the manager and wished her a happy birthday. She replied, "It is not my birthday. Last night was my first date since my divorce was final and my entire team felt it was an occasion to celebrate."

About two weeks later, I walked by her cubicle again and there was just one black balloon hanging up. When I asked the manager about it, she replied, "No, it was my second date and this guy was not a keeper." Although this example may not fit with the culture in your organization, everyone at AmRes showed that they cared about each other.

Honoring special days, whether it is a birthday, anniversary, new addition to the family, graduation, or promotion, tells people that they are special and valued.

> "The more you praise and celebrate your life, the more there is in life to celebrate."
> **OPRAH WINFREY**

Strategy 51. **Recognition is everyone's job**

Many organizations believe that recognition is the job of human resources. It is not! When organizations rely on that department to be the organization's sole motivator, they fail. Recognition that comes out of human resources is usually generic so it will work everywhere in the organization. Building an environment where everyone feels recognized and appreciated is everyone's job.

In the Best-of-the-Best organizations, it is the job of human resources to:

■ Measure the culture with an employee opinion survey and break out the results by department, branch, or location so every leader knows the reality of the culture in their area.

- Develop and make available different forms of recognition, such as toolkits that include articles on motivation and recognition, certificates that can be customized, gift certificates, gifts, or movie passes.
- Make sure managers are well-trained in the areas of leadership and supervision.
- Ensure managers have a working action plan, based on the results of the employee opinion survey, to create workplace excellence.

Making an effort to recognize someone's uniqueness goes a long way. All it takes is a brief note or phone call. Here is an example of a note received by a social worker in a hospital: "Thank you for all the support you have given to the families of patients in our unit. Your dedicated effort to ensure parents have their needs met gives us a lot more time to focus on the medical needs of the children. Your efforts are greatly appreciated."

Peer recognition works because it increases the overall frequency of recognition. When the frequency of recognition increases, people feel better and the environment becomes a much nicer place to work. The persuasive "law of reciprocation" grabs hold and becomes a positive force in the organization.

We all have had the experience of a person not on our list sending us a holiday card or showing up at the front door with a holiday gift. The "law of reciprocation" states that if I do something nice for you, even as simple as sending you a greeting card, you will feel a powerful need to reciprocate. The same law applies to the business of recognition and appreciation.

> **Building an environment where everyone feels recognized and appreciated is everyone's job.**

If I recognize or show appreciation for something you do, it increases the chances that you will return the appreciation or recognition to me. It is important to note that you had better genuinely mean your recognition and appreciation or the outcome will be worse than if you had not said anything to the recipient. When you don't mean it, your recognition or appreciation will not have the intended impact, but, rather, will come across as manipulation.

> "Kind words can be short and easy to speak, but their echoes are truly endless."
>
> **MOTHER TERESA**

Strategy 52. Be grateful for people support

When you look up *grateful* on dictionary.com, the word is defined as "appreciative of benefits received." When employees know you value their contributions and are truly grateful for the difference they make to the organization's success, they will ensure that great things happen. It does not matter if it is your boss, a direct report, or your significant other. When people feel valued, they are more motivated to help you achieve your goals.

The opposite of being grateful is not being appreciative for benefits received or taking people for granted. There are some managers who will say, "I do not take people for granted. I pay them well to show up and do their jobs, and that is what I expect them to do." We are in total agreement with this last comment. All employees who come to work are paid to show up and do their jobs. But, when you have this expectation that is exactly what you get: disengaged people who show up and do exactly what you pay them to do.

A leader who understands the importance of being grateful is Douglas R. Conant, CEO of the Campbell Soup Company. Since joining Campbell Soup in January 2001, Conant has sent more than 16,000 thank you notes to employees at all levels of the organization. Does being grateful help drive results? We think it does. Since March of 2003, Campbell Soup's stock is up 100%, more than double the results of other comparable food companies (*Business Week*, December 4, 2006).

Be grateful for the contributions of each team member. One participant in a seminar asked, "Do I need to be grateful for the one employee on our team who causes me the most amount of grief?" Another participant responded, "Be grateful. If every employee on your team were perfect, the team would not need you." So true!

> "Gratitude unlocks the fullness of life. It turns what we have into enough, and more. It turns denial into acceptance, chaos into order, confusion into clarity.... It turns problems into gifts, failures into success, the unexpected into perfect timing, and mistakes into important events. Gratitude makes sense of our past, brings peace for today, and creates a vision for tomorrow."
> **MELODIE BEATTIE**

Strategy 53. Kill the "employee of the month" award

This action is treading on sacred ground for many organizations, but we feel that the Employee of the Month, Employee of the Quarter, and Employee of the Year awards do more harm than good. That's because most organizations do not set hard, objective criteria to determine who deserves the award.

If companies stated objective criteria about exactly what it takes to win the award, there would be more than just one Employee of the Month. Or the same individuals would win the award each consecutive month because their results would be consistently the closest to being in alignment with the award criteria. This is like asking people to play a game while you make up the rules as you go. When people cannot figure out the rules to the game, they quickly lose interest in playing.

At the end of one strategic planning retreat, the vice president of human resources said, "We need to pick this month's Employee of the Month before we leave the retreat." Another vice president responded, "We need to pick a man this month because the last three winners have all been women." They finally selected a man who had not ever won the award. When the selection process relies on such subjectivity, it causes employees to ask questions like: Exactly what do I need to do to become the Employee of the Month? How is this month's winner any better than I am, especially when I have accomplished things even more significant than the winner? Am I not doing a good job?

Another organization took great pride in the Manager of the Quarter award. They actually paid a bonus of $10,000 to the winner. One manager told me, "I hope I do not win the award. It has such a stigma of being the 'kiss ass' of the quarter versus someone who is truly the top-performing manager in the organization." Imagine— $10,000 was not worth the stigma that was attached to a poorly designed award.

We recommend offering planned, spontaneous recognition when employees in the organization do great things. There may be five employees this month worthy of recognition; next month, there might not be any. When employees can connect significance to the recognition, it is a lot more meaningful.

> "Don't worry when you are not recognized, but strive to be worthy of recognition."
> **ABRAHAM LINCOLN**

KEY # 7: ACCOUNTABILITY COUNTS

It is virtually impossible to hold employees accountable for their performance if they are not clear on their performance expectations. According to 85.1% of employees at the Best-of-the-Best organizations, they work with clearly defined job descriptions. Even more (92.5%) believe they have a clear understanding of the performance standards/measurements at the company. Accountability for meeting the performance measures is delivered during performance reviews that help staff learn and improve—80.7% of employees at Best-of-the-Best organizations feel their reviews accomplish that—and through ongoing feedback throughout the year.

Strategy 54. Demand Unwavering Commitment

We are all for honest communication from employees. As a leader, you should encourage employees to tell you what they like and don't like about the organization and the department's goals. They should feel free to tell you when they believe you are wrong. They can even provide feedback on your leadership skills so you can "turn up the volume" to be more effective.

But once a decision is made for the organization or the team, then it is critical for your organization's success to demand unwavering commitment. While candid communication is important, exhibiting behaviors that undermine the achievement of goals should not be tolerated. What is amazing is how many leaders make excuses for their employees' lack of commitment. Some of the excuses we hear are:

- The employee has worked for the organization for a long period of time.
- The employee does not like change.
- The employee does a good job on the other technical aspects of the job.
- The boss is too busy to deal with the situation.
- The boss does not like conflict.
- The boss hopes that the employee will improve.

> When you demand unwavering commitment, remember that morale will usually decline before it can rise to an even higher level.

When you demand unwavering commitment, remember that morale will usually decline before it can rise to an even higher level. The reason that morale declines at first is because people do not like to be held accountable for a commitment to which they lack desire or agreement. If you stay the course and hold fast to your desire for commitment, eventually the behaviors will change and become aligned with the goals. When there is alignment of goals, results improve. When results improve, morale improves.

Demanding unwavering commitment to the organization's goals is not easy. The alternative is even more difficult. When employees do not exhibit the behaviors that actively demonstrate their support for the team's or organization's goals, they undermine workplace excellence. The lack of support for the goals undermines morale, as well as your success as a leader, and lengthens the amount of time it takes to accomplish the goals.

> "There's a difference between interest and commitment. When you're interested in doing something, you do it only when it's convenient. When you're committed to something, you accept no excuses, only results."
> **KEN BLANCHARD**

Strategy 55. Measure hard results

For the first few years of our consulting business, we focused on the soft side of leadership. In other words, we placed a high value on how people felt about their work experience. Our secondary focus was on the results that the organization achieved. This was a mistake.

Based on our employee opinion survey benchmarks that contain over 100,000 employees, the Best-of-the-Best companies taught us valuable leadership lessons: Focus on the hard, tangible results. Measure the hard, tangible results. Reward people for successfully achieving hard, tangible results. And, when the hard, tangible results meet or exceed expectations, morale takes care of itself.

The Best-of-the-Best organizations score over fifteen points higher than organizations in the Overall Benchmark in the hard, tangible areas of:

- Clarity of mission and vision
- Clarity of strategic direction
- Clarity of the organization's strategic goals

- Employees knowing exactly what goals they are responsible for achieving
- Holding employees accountable to defined performance standards

> "An ounce of performance is worth pounds of promises."
>
> **MAE WEST**

Strategy 56. Be fair! Hold everyone accountable for results

There is a big problem when your organization's culture is based on politics and who you know instead of a reputation for recognizing the performance of each employee. Many of us have worked in an organization where a coworker is worthless when it comes to serving and supporting others in the organization. This person should be fired. But someone in power in the organization, for whatever reason, protects the worthless wonder.

Each year, we do a 360-degree evaluation on each of our team members. One year, I (Jane) rated one of our employees a 5 out of 5 when it came to the area of teamwork. When I looked at the results of her 360-degree, the staff had rated her a 2 out of a possible 5. When I talked with the staff, I told them I was surprised because I thought this employee was a 5. One staff member responded, "She is a 5 to you and Peter. To everyone else she is a 1 or a 2." That frank feedback helped our team refine our performance review process to break the rating on teamwork into two questions. One question focused on teamwork and support to the senior consultants. The second question was focused on rating teamwork and support to fellow members of the staff.

When people are not held equally accountable for producing results, employees do not perceive the manager of the organization as being fair. Many times, managers tell us they do hold everyone accountable. Still, not all employees know what managers do one-on-one with employees to ensure accountability. This may be true, but it might not matter. The only things employees are able to observe and form an opinion on regarding accountability is the outcome or results of each employee's behavior.

When you begin to hold employees accountable, it is important to remember that morale may go down before it rises to a higher level. We call this riding the "J" curve of workplace excellence. When you start on the accountability trail, some employees may become resentful. If you are a new leader to a team, you know what this feels like. The employee wants to tell you something like this: "I liked my old boss a lot better. My old boss did not bug me and I didn't bug her. You annoy me, and I would be a whole lot happier if you would just leave me alone."

When you start to hold employees like this accountable, they, along with every other marginal employee, become disgruntled. Morale declines and starts to move toward the bottom of the "J" curve. The

THE J-CURVE

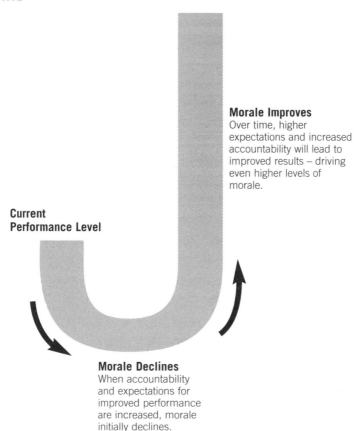

Morale Improves
Over time, higher expectations and increased accountability will lead to improved results – driving even higher levels of morale.

Current Performance Level

Morale Declines
When accountability and expectations for improved performance are increased, morale initially declines.

morale and motivation must go down to the starting point on the "J" before it can rise up to the top.

Being a great leader in search of the path that leads to workplace excellence is not for the faint of heart. Holding all employees accountable to clearly defined outcomes is hard work. With really difficult employees, it feels like a fight. Yet holding everyone accountable and holding onto the "J" for the entire ride takes you one step closer to creating workplace excellence.

> "The reason people blame things on others is that there's really only one other choice."
>
> **JANE FLAHERTY**

Strategy 57. **Take responsibility!**

Up until his untimely death in July of 2006, Ken Lay, the former CEO of Enron, claimed ignorance about the depth of Enron's financial problem and blamed the severity of the problems on some rogue managers at lower levels in the organization.

Several of the major airlines, with the exception of Southwest, blame their lack of profitability on September 11, the price of fuel, and too much competition.

In a 2004 study of annual reports, Fiona Lee of the University of Michigan and Larissa Tiedens of Stanford found that stock prices were higher one year later when companies blamed poor performance on controllable internal factors rather than on external issues. They analyzed twenty-one years' worth of "Letters to the Shareholders" in annual reports for fourteen companies in three industries: pharmaceuticals, food and beverages, and industrial equipment. By hypothetically picking stocks based on how managers explained negative performance (self-blaming vs. other-blaming), the researchers found the stocks of the five most self-blaming companies yielded an adjusted return of 14%–19% more than the stocks of the five most other-blaming companies.

Excuses are also an ineffective customer service strategy; they tend to upset customers and make bad situations even worse. Admitting a mistake and correcting the problem increases the chances of a customer returning and doing business with you again. Your customers are loyal because they trust that when there is a problem, your company will take responsibility and correct the problem (*Business 2.0*, April 1, 2006).

Howard Schultz, Starbucks founder and CEO, is a leader who knows how to take responsibility for mistakes. When Starbucks missed its sales and profit expectations in 2007, Schultz could have blamed the lack of sales and profits on the economy, the time of year, or even the consumer price index. Instead, in an interview with Andy Serwer, Schultz stated, "I want to be clear that I take full responsibility for where our company is now and also for where it will be going forward" (*Fortune Magazine*, February 4, 2008; pg.14).

Another CEO who knows the importance of taking responsibility is Blair Sadler, the retired CEO of Rady Children's Hospital, San Diego. In March 2006, the unthinkable happened at Rady Children's Hospital. Within a period of about two weeks, two employees were accused of either molesting children or being in possession of child pornography. The 2,800 employees and 750 physicians at Children's, the very people who dedicated their lives to protecting children from harm, were devastated. In this situation, some leaders may have tried to minimize the story or put a positive spin on the news.

Instead, Sadler held a news conference with San Diego's Police Chief William Lansdowne and said, "Our hiring standards require extensive criminal background checks on all new employees and volunteers. We require and provide annual training on child-abuse prevention, identification, and reports for all staff, every three months." Sadler went on to state that these numerous safeguards at the hospital apparently were not enough to prevent what occurred (*San Diego Union-Tribune*, March 10, 2006).

Everyone makes mistakes and things do happen that are outside your sphere of control. But what everyone knows is that excuses stink. Taking responsibility for your department or organization's problems shows great leadership. When leaders admit mistakes and problems and provide a clear strategy to resolve the problem, employees find it easier to respect and follow the person who has control over the outcome. When employees hear leaders complain that problems are externally controlled, it is hard for them to gain motivation to fix something over which, no matter what they do, they have no control. Apologize, take ownership, and take responsibility to fix the problem.

"Accountability breeds response-ability."
STEPHEN R. COVEY

Strategy 58. Resolve conflicts quickly

There are some consultants who make their entire living conducting seminars on conflict resolution. There is a reason for this. The cultures of some organizations avoid resolving conflicts. In these organizations, conflict becomes a big "un-discussable." Everyone will talk about the disagreement one-on-one, but no one has the courage to call a meeting, put the conflict in the middle of the table, and discuss it with the people who can come up with an agreeable solution.

The conflict consultants tell us disagreement can be good if, for example, it brings together people who do not see eye-to-eye and the outcome is a stronger relationship and a better solution. We agree. We also believe that the only good conflict in organizations is the one that gets resolved quickly.

Whether it is two team members who are not on the same page, or two departments going head-to-head, if the conflict is resolved promptly, it is good. If the conflict lingers on, a huge amount of time is wasted since people's energies are focused on peripheral issues that are not productive to creating organizational success.

When an organizational assessment reveals there is unresolved conflict, the people promoting the conflict are like different teams competing in a league. Neither wins. The only team that is really winning in this league is their competitor.

To resolve conflicts quickly, you will find it helpful to:

Force communication. When there is conflict, most people would rather avoid going head-on to discuss the situation. Setting up a meeting as quickly as possible is the first step.

Meet face-to-face. There are some people who will walk a mile around the office to complain about someone who sits right next to them. Or they send a nasty e-mail. In resolving conflict, face-to-face is better.

Develop options. The most difficult people to deal with in the world are unilateral thinkers. We know them as the "my way or the highway" folks. If there are two or three options, most times you can reach resolution.

Use your organization's vision as a guidepost. When in conflict, don't lose sight of your organization's vision. Often, it will serve as a compass to focus your discussions and possible resolutions to the problem being addressed. Keep discussions open, considering multiple alternatives.

Agree on next actions. It is important to leave this discussion with actions or next steps in place.

Follow-up. Before you end the meeting, set up the next meeting to discuss what went well or right since the first meeting and identify any course corrections that need to be made.

> "You can't shake hands with a clenched fist."
> **INDIRA GANDHI**

TIP

Got a conflict that is giving you a headache? We've got just what you need. Go to www.peterstark.com, and enter the word ENGAGE in the Tip Box.

Strategy 59. **Give gossipers and whiners more work**

If there is one thing that can kill an environment that promotes workplace excellence, it is gossipers who spend a large portion of their time spreading ill will. Gossipers usually do not spend time talking positively about others and the organization. Instead they gossip about how good things used to be in the past. They gripe about how current decisions are wrong for the organization. They criticize team members' inadequacies and mistakes.

> **When it comes to gossipers and whiners, it is important to focus on the real problem.**

When it comes to gossipers and whiners, it is important to focus on the real problem. The focus is not the unhappy employees going around wasting their, and everyone else's, time gossiping. The concern is how much time these discontents have on their hands in the first place. The real problem is managers who do not give gossipers and whiners enough work to do and then don't hold them accountable to high performance and the completion of all work that is assigned to them.

If you keep increasing the workload every time someone finds the time to gossip, one of three things is going to happen: (1) the gossipers are going to run out of time to gossip and get the job done; (2) the gossipers will get so frustrated and angry that they now have to work they will quit; or (3) the gossipers will be coached and counseled out of the organization on accountability issues. With any of these outcomes, you are one step closer to workplace excellence. Every time you see or hear someone gossiping or whining, remember this: the person does not have enough work to do.

> "Gossip is a sort of smoke that comes from the dirty tobacco pipes of those who diffuse it: it proves nothing but the bad taste of the smoker."
> **GEORGE ELIOT**

Strategy 60. Deal with bullies or abusive people in the organization

Number one on the list of stupid behaviors is the inability to control emotions. Whether it is anger, moodiness, or inappropriate responses to everyday situations, emotional people come across as bullies, either passively or actively, and they are mentally abusive to others in the organization. Our clients recognize that these individuals are a threat to a culture of workplace excellence and put a stop to these inappropriate behaviors in one of two ways.

First, in most of these situations, our clients hire a coach to help the bullies learn better ways to communicate with others in the organization. We have learned that about 50% of the people we coach change their behaviors and become even stronger contributors to the organization's success. These leaders embrace the coach's suggestions and are active learners in becoming more effective leaders. We've also learned that the other 50% exhibit what we refer to as Popeye Syndrome (see page 86).

These individuals do not feel responsible for their own behaviors, much less their impact on others. They are proud of themselves and their past results. Because these individuals are unwilling to change and they say, "I am what I am," many of the Popeye Syndrome managers end up being fired after several months of working with the coach. In most of these instances, these individuals view the coaching process as punitive or remedial. In the relationship with the coach, these individuals hold one, nonverbalized goal: "What do I have to do or say to get this executive coach out of my life?"

Amazing as it sounds, we have worked with executives, whose annual salaries exceeded $700,000, who lost their jobs because they were unwilling to change.

The second alternative our clients take is giving the dysfunctional bully an ultimatum that goes something like, "You either agree to change your behavior or sign a separation agreement."

Most bullies or abusive people in organizations earn a reputation for producing spectacular results. That is why they are more difficult to deal with than a poor performer. With a weak performer who is an abusive bully, it is an easy decision. You fire the person as quickly as possible. It is a much more difficult decision when the bully is a top-producing individual. Organizations that build a reputation for workplace excellence recognize that both results—and how they are produced   are critical for the organization's success.

> "Courage is fire, and bullying is smoke."
> **BENJAMIN DISRAELI**

Strategy 61. Enforce the company's policy on harassment

As we head toward the year 2010, we keep thinking that harassment will no longer be an issue in organizations. Wrong! Each year, some of the nation's leading law firms refer to us for coaching leaders who have been accused of harassment. While it comes in many forms, most instances of harassment are revealed by behaviors that are not welcomed by others in the workplace. Disrespectful behaviors have always been wrong. They are still wrong today. If you are a manager who is harassing another team member, the company will always be liable and in many states, you could be held personally liable. The Best-of-the-Best organizations and leaders state a policy of zero tolerance when it comes to harassment.

It is worth noting that as the workforce becomes younger, more and more people will bring a stronger understanding of what harassment means. Nowadays, in the first year of middle school, students learn that while flirting may be welcome, unwanted harassment is not. These new workers may know the laws better than many seasoned managers.

However, you should not enforce the company's policy on harassment only because you might be sued. Rather, enforce the policy because it is the right thing to do and because your goal is to create an environment where all employees can give their optimal performance.

> "When people honor each other, there is a trust established that leads to synergy, interdependence, and deep respect. Both parties make decisions and choices based on what is right, what is best, what is valued most highly."
> **BLAINE LEE**

Strategy 62. Don't be held hostage

When an inadequate performer threatens to quit, which seldom happens, the decision to accept the offer is an easy one to make. The decision is much more difficult when the threat comes from a top performer. What should you do when you have a top performer who is exceedingly difficult to work with?

When it comes to results on a scale of one to ten (with one representing low and ten, high), these top performers get a ten. They get the job done and the results are spectacular. The challenge is that they leave a wake of "debris" as they pass and it splashes up on everyone. As the leader, you deal with constant complaints from these top performers' direct reports, peers, and sometimes even a customer. Although the top performers may be a little arrogant, demanding, or even abrasive at times, you make excuses for them because you don't have to worry about their results.

One more thing about these high performers: Every time you try to hold them accountable for how they treat and interact with people, they blame others and threaten to quit. So you start to dance around these difficult people in hopes that you can convince them to stay. Perhaps you even contemplate hiring an executive coach to help smooth over the rough edges. Most of the time, your gut tells you that these behaviors need to change, but your head makes excuses because these team members are so good at the technical aspects of the job. When you fall into this trap and start to make excuses, even to the point of trying to talk them out of quitting, you need to have your business cards reprinted with a new title: Hostage.

Most people who are difficult to deal with and who threaten to quit seldom do. There is a reason these troublesome people don't leave the organization. Deep down inside, they know they are tough to deal with and the next company they join may not be so tolerant of their abusive behaviors. They have fewer options for future employment because everyone who has ever worked with them never wants to work with them again.

So here is the lesson. Don't be held hostage. If people threaten to quit, you can assume they are not happy with your organization or the specific changes you are proposing that they make. When people are not happy and are difficult to work with, an excellent work environment cannot take root. Let these individuals know that leaving the organization is a real possibility and if they are unwilling to make the changes in behavior you are discussing, you are willing to help them transition to another organization.

The new person you hire will not be making everyone's life miserable. The new person will have only two questions for you and the team: (1) "What do you need me to do?" and (2) "How soon do you need me to accomplish the task or goal?" When you can finally remove the word *Hostage* from your business cards, you will once again be able to say, "I love my job."

> "Whatever course you decide upon, there is always someone to tell you that you are wrong. There are always difficulties arising which tempt you to believe that your critics are right. To map out a course of action and follow it to an end requires courage."
>
> **RALPH WALDO EMERSON**

Strategy 63. Share your poorest performers with a competitor

People with performance problems deserve four things from their boss and the organization:

- Clearly defined performance goals
- Timely feedback if the goals are not being achieved
- Crystal clear knowledge of the consequences if the performance does not improve in a specific time frame
- Support to help the poor performance improve by, for example, training or mentoring

The question that leaders ask is, "What happens when you have done the above four steps, sometimes in multiple rounds, and the employee still does not improve?" If the employee remains a poor performer, here is a tip to help construct an even more positive, effective workplace: Share this person with a competitor.

There is no greater strategic action than to take your worst-performing employee and give that person the opportunity to undermine the teamwork, productivity, quality, and customer service at someone else's company, preferably your toughest competitor.

Why don't more leaders practice the strategy of sharing their poorest performers with a competitor? Many leaders "hope" that their inadequate performers will improve. When "hope" does not work, some leaders will try a "hint." When "hope" and "hint" do not work, they often resort to prayer. Difficult employees usually do not respond well to hope, hint, or prayer. They do respond well when they watch a leader in the organization effectively and swiftly deal with weak performance. Most leaders in this new situation only regret one thing, which is that they did not share the poor performer with a top competitor much sooner.

> "Some difficult employees are like wheelbarrows. Easily upset, they are
> only useful when pushed by someone else."
> **PETER BARRON STARK**

Strategy 64. Smash the time clock

Most organizations develop a corporate culture that tells people how many hours they need to be on-site working. Hourly employees are given clearly identified start and stop times. In every organization, there will always be people who are assigned specific times they need to be at work. Customers expect to be served and supported when the business is open, and the employees who serve them will always be accountable to be at work during a specific time.

But, in every organization there are positions where it does not matter when the work gets started as long as the desired end result is achieved and the work is completed on time. To create workplace excellence, set high expectations and focus on the results of the individual, not the hour hand on the time clock.

In most organizations, if you do not show up for work you are going to be fired. Best Buy, one of the nation's largest electronics retailers, has implemented a policy called ROWE at their Minneapolis headquarters. ROWE stands for "Results Oriented Work Environment." In putting ROWE into practice, Best Buy is trying to change from an environment of working long hours under stress to an environment that emphasizes results. In other words, Best Buy is smashing the time clock by realizing it is not the number of hours an employee spends at the office that counts, but rather, what that person produces. If you wish to adopt the ROWE philosophy, we recommend four steps to success.

First, both managers and employees need to be clear on what results are needed and when those results are due.

Second, increase communication among the manager, employee, and the team. When you are out of sight, it is easy to let up on communicating with each other. Use the abundant technology available today to stay in touch and keep current. Practice the concept of "no surprises" and overcommunicate so everyone stays connected.

Third, hold consistent team meetings, either by phone or in the office. It is critical that the team does not become a group of individuals all doing their own thing.

Fourth, managers need to recognize that a ROWE may not be applicable to every employee. Some people are self-motivated producers and in reality don't even need a manager. Others, without strong oversight, will mess up the "R" part of the ROWE. Hold everyone accountable and this new policy offers a great opportunity for even more employees to say, "I love my job!"

> "Don't tell people how to do things. Tell them what to do and let them surprise you with their results.
>
> GENERAL GEORGE S. PATTON

Strategy 65. Do the right thing!

Former congressman Duke Cunningham, an eight-term legislator from San Diego, California, went to prison in March, 2006 for taking over

$2,400,000 in bribes from federal contractors. Cunningham either asked the contractors for money in return for lobbying for contracts that would benefit them, or he was offered money in return for the favors. In February, 2007, Brent Wilkes, the Poway, California, businessman who owned a company that contracted with the United States government, was indicted and found guilty of bribing Cunningham. Federal prosecutors recommended Wilkes be sentenced to a sixty-year prison term. Cunningham and the contractors had the opportunity to say no and do the right thing. They chose not to.

One public servant who did do the right thing, even when it cost him and the City of New York big time, was New York's past mayor, Rudy Giuliani. After the 9/11 terrorist attacks, a Saudi prince, Alwaleed Bin Talal Bin Abdul Aziz Alsaud, toured Ground Zero and then wrote a check to the City of New York for $10,000,000. Most cities and their mayors would be excited anytime someone gave them a check for $10,000,000. The trouble was, the prince also included a press release with his donation. The press release stated:

> "However, at times like this one, we must address some of the issues that led to such a criminal attack. I believe the government of the United States of America should re-examine its policies in the Middle East and adopt a more balanced stance toward the Palestinian cause. Our Palestinian brethren continue to be slaughtered at the hands of Israelis while the world turns the other cheek."

The mayor, who had been told of the press release just moments before his daily briefing but after receiving the check, was visibly annoyed by it. "I entirely reject that statement," he said. "That's totally contrary to what I said at the United Nations," he added, referring to his address to the international body (*New York Times*, October 12, 2001). As hard as it must have been to turn away that much money, Giuliani told the prince to take his $10,000,000 and shove it sideways up his oil rig.

Regardless of what situation you may find yourself and/or your firm mired in, there is never an excuse for violating your own principles and morals or for breaking the law. In effect, there is never a right time to do the wrong thing.

"The time is always right to do what is right."

MARTIN LUTHER KING JR.

Strategy 66. Swim with the dolphins

When it comes to achieving performance, there are four types of workers who, amazingly enough, mimic the behaviors of sea creatures: dolphins, cross-eyed dogfish, carp, and sharks.

Dolphins. Whether they swim with sharks, carp, or cross-eyed dogfish, dolphins are incredibly effective at producing top-quality results. And they achieve those results by living the company's values. Dolphins are always thinking ahead, planning their next strategy. They learn from, and respond appropriately to, their rapidly changing environment. You know what to do with dolphins. You want to give them even more responsibility in the organization and if you could find more dolphins, you would hire them.

Cross-eyed dogfish. Dogfish are ineffective at producing results. They don't get their own jobs done but are really good at creating more work for others in the organization. If that were not enough, cross-eyed dogfish are not even nice. Difficult to get along with as a team member, they are also low on character. You do not trust that they will do what they say they are going to do. Cross-eyed dogfish set low personal standards and then consistently fail to achieve them. You also know what to do with the cross-eyed dogfish. Fire them and hire a dolphin!

Carp. Really nice organizations struggle with the question, "What do you do with the carp?" A challenge because they do not produce significant results, carp are really pleasant and people in the organization like them. In fact, if you let a carp go, there are always other carp who talk about how much the organization is changing for the worse. A carp's favorite lines, when a fellow carp is let go, are, "Our organization used to be like a family" and, "We used to care about people." With carp, you want to coach, counsel, and train. If that does not work, make a hard decision. Share the carp with a competitor who values really nice easy-going, ineffective employees.

Sharks. Sharks are the most difficult employees to fire because no one likes to sacrifice anyone who produces. The challenge with sharks is how they achieve their results. Sharks do not live the organization's values, much less follow the character behaviors of positive leaders. A favorite line of a shark is, "I am paid to do a job." Sharks will do whatever it takes, including running over people or compromising ethics, to get the job done. Like carp, sharks need to be coached, counseled, and retrained. You don't want to lose their results, but how they achieve them has a big impact on organizational excellence. Unfortunately, if the coaching and counseling do not work, sharks need to go.

To be successful in effectively managing performance, you need to let the cross-eyed dogfish go and hire more dolphins. These are easy decisions that need to be made quickly. With the carps and sharks, you need to coach, counsel, and train. To create excellence in the workplace, other employees must either see positive changes in the shark and carp behaviors or watch those colleagues swim away.

> "Learn to adjust yourself to the conditions you have to endure, but make a point of trying to alter or correct conditions so that they are most favorable to you."
> **WILLIAM FREDERICK BOOK**

TIP

Want to think like a dolphin? Figure out how to deal with a shark? Go to www.peterstark.com, and enter the word ENGAGE in the Tip Box.

KEY # 8: EVERY EMPLOYEE LEARNS AND GROWS

We have already shown that Best-of-the-Best organizations are better at defining job responsibilities and performance measurements than other organizations. Their leaders do a finer job of providing constructive feedback to employees about their performance. The ingredients that bind these concepts together are the training program that prepares people to do their job, and the professional development that enables them to go above and beyond it. Not only do 84.1% of the staff at the Best-of-the-Best companies believe their organizations have a good training program, 86.3% believe the training improves their job skills. Their recognition of the company's support of their careers is such that 83.3% believe there is a career opportunity at their workplace in the next three years.

Strategy 67. Ensure everyone has a growth and development plan

We feel strongly that every employee in your organization needs a plan in order to learn and grow. Most people find that when they are learning and growing, they are more motivated. When employees feel stagnant in their jobs they usually feel that their growth is stunted. Each year, put specific learning and growth goals on paper, both for you and each of your direct reports.

It is important to ask your employees to define their growth goals. It may include formal training or cross-training with another employee or department, or it could mean taking a course at a local college. If employees are not involved in defining the learning and growth goals, they tend to feel less empowered in the process. When people do not feel empowered, they lose motivation.

"The growth and development of people is the highest calling of leadership."
HARVEY S. FIRESTONE

Strategy 68. **Be a mentor**

Every year, hundreds of organizations start the process to begin a mentor or succession-planning program. The purpose of the programs—to develop talent—is awesome.

The worst programs we have ever been involved with were the ones that made formal assignments of mentor and protégé. The organization's human resources or organizational development departments prescribed exactly what needed to happen in the program, including how many times the mentor and protégé should meet on an annual basis. The protégé felt like an intruder into the mentor's busy schedule, while the mentor felt compelled to give the mentee some quality time. The mentor would ask, "What can I do to help you in your career?" After one hour of forced communication, both participants crossed the meeting off of their to-do lists.

The best mentor programs are informal philosophies where organizations place a high value on helping people to grow and develop, both personally and professionally. When the leaders in the organization put into action the value of helping people to grow and develop, being a mentor works incredibly well.

For instance, a leader takes a subordinate to a Toastmasters' meeting because she believes that improved communication skills will help the employee's career. Another invites a peer or subordinate to a meeting he would never be asked to attend on his own. Or, a mentor gives an employee a project that stretches her current capabilities. These are examples of leaders who truly care about the success of someone else in the organization.

> "If you are given a chance to be a role model, I think you should always take it because you can influence a person's life in a positive light, and that's what I want to do. That's what it's all about."
> **TIGER WOODS**

Strategy 69. Continuously delegate increased responsibility

To find the time needed to focus on "cool stuff" and create an environment that produces significant results, you need to continuously delegate. Delegation frees you up from tactical tasks and allows you to concentrate on the strategic work that leads to innovation. Delegation also helps your team members grow.

To be effective at delegating, two dynamics come into play. The first action to effectively delegate a task or responsibility to another is that you need to trust people, and you will especially need to trust that specific person. Trust is one of the qualities that distinguishes the Best-of-the-Best leaders. (You can follow the steps to building trusting relationships listed in chapter three.) Second, you have to have confidence that if something does go wrong, you have the ability to correct any situation. Trust in others and confidence in yourself—these are the two key actions for effective delegating.

In his autobiography, *My American Journey,* Colin Powell tells a story about how President Reagan once signed a photograph of Powell briefing the president in the Oval Office. At the bottom of the photo, Reagan wrote, "If you say so, Colin, it must be right."

> "No man will make a great leader who wants to do it all himself or get all the credit."
> ANDREW CARNEGIE

Strategy 70. Be a Pygmalion—believe in people

Whether you trust that people on your team are capable of doing the job, or do not trust that people are capable of doing the job, you are right! In Greek mythology a sculptor, Pygmalion, sought to carve an ivory statue of the ideal woman. The statue, which he named Galatea, was so beautiful that Pygmalion fell desperately in love with his own creation. He prayed to the goddess Venus to bring Galatea to life. Venus granted his prayer and the couple lived happily ever after.

Inspired, George Bernard Shaw wrote a play called *Pygmalion*. In Shaw's play, which was made into the Broadway musical and movie *My Fair Lady*, snobbish phonetics professor Henry Higgins wagers that he can take a Cockney flower girl, Eliza Doolittle, and, with some vigorous training, present her in high society as a duchess. Higgins succeeds.

But a key point lies in a comment by Eliza to Higgins's friend Colonel Pickering: "You see, really and truly, apart from the things anyone can pick up (the dressing and the proper way of speaking and so on), the difference between a lady and a flower girl is not how she behaves, but how she's treated. I shall always be a flower girl to Professor Higgins, because he always treats me as a flower girl, and always will. But I know I can be a lady to you because you always treat me as a lady, and always will."

In organizations, the Pygmalion effect is the recognition that your expectations of an individual can radically influence that individual's behavior and perceived performance. This is the actual reason why the best mentor-protégé relationship occurs when the mentor believes that the protégé can rise to an even higher level in the organization and the mentor goes out of the way to ensure that the protégé succeeds. If you trust that someone can do the job, you tend to pass along increased responsibilities and share knowledge to help the individual grow and develop.

> "Whether you think you can or whether you think you can't, you're right."
> **HENRY FORD**

KEY # 9: PROBLEMS ... NO PROBLEM!

If you are a customer with a problem that a company resolves quickly and cheerfully, aren't you more likely to be loyal to that organization? The Best-of-the-Best companies believe this is true, as evidenced by the powerful statement that 90% of their staff members believe their companies want them to solve problems. (In comparison, only 73% of the employees in the Overall Benchmark feel their companies want them to be problem solvers.) Both internal and external problems can be solved with a staff of innovators who quickly grasp the issue and then take action. That's an environment of workplace excellence that motivates staff and customers.

Strategy 71. Empower employees

Webster's Dictionary defines *empower* as "to give official authority." Real empowerment means giving employees the information they require to make decisions without having to go to a supervisor or manager for approval. To be fully empowered, employees need the accountability, responsibility, and authority to make a decision.

Enlightened organizations do just that. One example is at the Sheraton Universal Hotel in Universal City, California, where the front desk manager has the complete authority to provide upgrades or discounts to solve customer problems.

A famous example of an organization that empowers employees is Nordstrom. New employees are given a copy of the famous Nordstrom Employee Handbook—a single 5 x 8-inch gray card containing 75 words:

WELCOME TO NORDSTROM

We're glad to have you with our Company. Our number one goal is to provide outstanding customer service. Set both your personal and professional goals high. We have great confidence in your ability to achieve them.

Nordstrom Rules: Rule #1: Use your good judgment in all situations. There will be no additional rules.

Please feel free to ask your department manager, store manager, or division general manager any question at any time.

The handbook clearly tells employees they have one goal, to do whatever it takes to make customers happy. Other organizations say the words, but will not let employees act on them. Their empowerment reaches as far as "You are empowered as long as you don't make a decision." Or, "Before you make the decision, ask me." Or worse, "Why did you make that decision? Now you are in big trouble."

When we ask employees if they have the ability to make decisions to improve quality or solve customer problems, 85% of the employees in the Best-of-the-Best Benchmark responded favorably that they do. The companies in the Overall Benchmark scored an approximately 79% favorable response. The data in both benchmarks tell us that companies who care about what their employees think will work hard to empower them to take responsibility and make the right decisions.

In today's challenging business environment, employee empowerment can improve the level of customer service and provide management with time to run the business and make important strategic decisions.

> "The best executive is the one who has sense enough to pick good men to
> do what he wants done, and self-restraint enough to keep from meddling
> with them while they do it."
> THEODORE ROOSEVELT

Strategy 72. Identify and handle problems quickly

Most organizations are great at identifying problems. What separates the Best-of-the-Best organizations is that they are quick to fix problems. An example of this became apparent when we worked with a major league sports franchise. The three months prior to the opening of the season, people in the ball club were commenting that attendance for the first three games was not going to meet the budgeted goals.

The first three games came and went. Despite fireworks and a giveaway, attendance was way below expectations. In an interview, one employee stated that the club's previous president would have called a meeting two months prior to the start of the season and facilitated a cross-departmental action plan of how to boost attendance.

The Best-of-the-Best leaders have an attitude about problems, which is that problems give leaders a purpose. If there were no problems, there is a good chance the leader would not be needed. As one person said, "The only people who have no problems are dead people." If you look at that comment from the opposite side of the fence, the more problems you have, the more alive you are! When they are resolved quickly, problems make an organization even stronger

As a leader, it is imperative that you take charge and facilitate a solution to problems that threaten the operation and productivity of your particular organization. It is extremely important that you first listen carefully when a direct report and/or colleague comes to you with an issue, then investigate for yourself and prepare to take effective action.

Given the incredibly competitive marketplace, you must prevent an apparently miniscule problem from snowballing out of control into a potentially organization-killing monster.

> "The 'how' thinker gets problems solved effectively because he wastes no time with futile 'ifs' but goes right to work on the creative 'how'."
> **NORMAN VINCENT PEALE**

KEY # 10: IT'S ALL ABOUT THE CUSTOMER

It would be difficult in today's world to find a company that admitted to being indifferent about customer service. After all, service is the special quality that positions one organization higher than others in the minds of their customers. Service attracts loyal customers, who ultimately link in the bottom line. A substantial 94.3% of employees at Best-of the-Best organizations report that their companies place a high value on customer service. But, showing that the organization also walks the talk, 89% say their company's policies and procedures enable them to provide high-quality service. That support is the appreciable difference between a good company and a great Best-of-the-Best company.

Strategy 73. Create policies and procedures that better serve both the needs of your customers and your staff

For decades, the Department of Motor Vehicles (DMV) in California upheld a reputation for being a bureaucratic nightmare of stationary lines. There was a line for getting a driver's license, a line for taking the test, and another line for obtaining a copy of your driving record. There was a separate line for anything you could possibly want from the DMV. The amazing thing about all these lines is that they were designed for one purpose: the convenience of the staff at the DMV. There is nothing convenient for the customer about standing in multiple lines to get various tasks accomplished.

A second frustrating policy of the DMV, right behind the multiple lines, was scheduling all its employees to take their lunch break between 11:30 AM and 1:00 PM. Yes, we all agree that this is the designated lunch time, but these are the exact times that most people are able to go the DMV to be served.

To be fair, today you can call the DMV and actually schedule an appointment to get your vehicle needs accomplished. The appointment may not be the equivalent of a personal shopping experience at Nordstrom, but it is better than wasting a good portion of your day standing in line.

When organizations design new policies that are convenient for the customer, many times—in the beginning stages of implementation—the new policies are difficult for the staff to master. With time, staff members find that they like working with happy customers even better, and the new policies become routine. Designing policies and procedures with the customer in mind helps create workplace excellence.

Remember: The number-one goal is to create an environment where employees love to come to work and customers love to do business. Designing policies that are flexible to meet the needs of your workforce and customers is critical for your organization's success. It is difficult to please customers if the employees delivering the service are not engaged. Policies allowing part-time employment, flexible hours, telecommuting, or job-sharing may help engage a workforce that is even more motivated to meet the needs of customers. When it comes to producing results, there are some part-time employees who can out-produce someone working full-time.

We are moving into an environment where there will be a shortage of well-qualified employees. Establishing policies that meet the needs of employees and developing relationships that build loyal customers will help organizations be even more successful in the future.

> "Customers don't expect you to be perfect. They do expect you to fix
> things when they go wrong."
> **DONALD PORTER**

Strategy 74. **Stop beating a dead horse**

Mary Bradley, a veteran respiratory therapist on the Rady Children's Hospital's well-regarded Advanced Life Support team, brought a stuffed pony that was about two feet tall to a team meeting. When the team started to rehash and complain about an issue for the umpteenth time, she tossed the pony into the middle of the room, gave team members a stick, and said, "If we can't get over this, then we need to beat this dead horse one more time." Since no one on the team wanted to be the one beating a dead horse, the team refocused on what actions they needed to take to improve the situation. Most times, when people are beating a dead horse, they have lost sight of both the customer and the vision.

To repeatedly bring up a particular topic with no chance of affecting the outcome is beating a dead horse. It is an action with no purpose because no matter how hard or how long you beat a dead horse, it is not going to get up and run. Unfortunately, some people cannot stop themselves.

For those team members, we sourced the Internet and customized twenty-six new strategies you should try.

1. Some horses are really strong willed. Buy a stronger whip!
2. Maybe it is the rider who is dead. Change riders!
3. Says things like, "This is the way we have always ridden this horse."
4. Appoint a committee to study the horse and make recommendations to revive it, like: "We need to put some lipstick on this pig."
5. Arrange to visit other organizations to see how they ride dead horses.
6. Increase the standards to ride dead horses.
7. Get teams to argue about nonissues that take the focus off the dead horse.
8. Get the organizational development team to institute a mandatory training session to increase our riding capacity.
9. Get a strong leader in the company to make a speech and state, "This horse will never die on my watch."
10. Change the requirements to prove that, "This horse is not dead."
11. Hire contractors or consultants who lack business knowledge to ride the dead horse.
12. Harness several dead horses together to give the perception of increased power and speed.
13. Declare that, "No horse is too dead to beat."
14. Provide additional funding to increase the horse's "functional life."
15. Do a Cost-Benefit Analysis to see if contractors can ride the horse cheaper.
16. Write a proposal to find the lowest price consultant to do CPR on the horse.
17. Buy a commercial off-the-shelf dead horse. No sense inventing a new dead horse.
18. Purchase a product to make dead horses run faster.
19. Declare the horse is now "better, faster, and cheaper."
20. Form a brainstorming session, where every idea is valued, to find new uses for dead horses.
21. Empower employees to bring the dead horse back to life.
22. BRAC (Base Realignment and Closure) the horse farm on which the dead horse was born.
23. Promote the dead horse to a management position so more dead horses can be rewarded.
24. Rename the dead horse "Paradigm Shift" and keep riding it for a few more years.
25. Tell people they need to "get out of the box" and ride the dead horse "smarter" not "harder."
26. Get the Information Technology Help Desk team involved. They will tell you to

reboot your dead horse with a Control-Alt-Delete maneuver. Don't be surprised if the horse momentarily comes alive again, until you retry the identical task that killed the horse the first time and triggered the call to the Help Desk.

If all these strategies fail, hire a consultant to help the team create a powerful positive vision of your customers happily riding dead horses, with all four legs sticking straight up in the air, for many years to come.

> "The single most important thing to remember about any enterprise is that there are no results inside its walls. The result of a business is a satisfied customer."
>
> **PETER DRUCKER**

Strategy 75. **Recognize the customer is not always right**

Gordon Bethune left the Boeing Company in 1994 to become president and CEO of Continental Airlines, at the time the fifth-largest airline in the United States. When Bethune took over, Continental, losing $55,000,000 per month, was widely recognized in the industry as providing the worst service of the country's ten largest airlines, and was on the verge of declaring bankruptcy for the third time in a decade. Within two years, Continental had turned around, posting the first of eleven straight quarters of record profits, and consistently ranking among the best airlines in customer satisfaction surveys.

Bethune's emphasis in turning Continental Airlines around, as explained in his bestseller, *From Worst to First*, was in satisfying customers and employees and ensuring that both groups remained happy with how Continental treated them. However, Bethune also made it clear that the cliché "the customer is always right" philosophy didn't always apply at Continental, and that when conflicts arose between employees and abusive customers, he would side with employees:

> When we run into customers that we can't reel back in, our loyalty is with our employees. They have to put up with this stuff every day. Just because you

buy a ticket does not give you the right to abuse our employees.... We run more than three million people through our books every month. One or two of those people are going to be unreasonable, demanding jerks. When it's a choice between supporting your employees, who work with you every day and make your product what it is, or some irate jerk who demands a free ticket to Paris because you ran out of peanuts, whose side are you going to be on? You can't treat your employees like serfs. You have to value them.... If they think that you won't support them when a customer is out of line, even the smallest problem can cause resentment.

GORDON BETHUNE

FORMER CEO, CONTINENTAL AIRLINES

Bethune shared in his book how he unconditionally supported a flight attendant offended by a passenger's child wearing a hat with Nazi and KKK emblems on it and asked the man to put the hat away. The passenger was very upset, and he followed up with multiple nasty letters and even a visit to Continental's headquarters. No amount of customer service could appease him. As Bethune concluded, "He bought a ticket on our airplane, and that means we'll take him where he wants to go. But if he's going to be rude and offensive, he's welcome to fly another airline."

Herb Kelleher, one of the founders of Southwest Airlines, has gone on record with the philosophy that supporting one's employees is more important than catering to abusive customers. An example of Kelleher putting his philosophy into action is found in *Nuts! Southwest Airlines' Crazy Recipe for Business and Personal Success* by our good friends, Kevin and Jackie Freiberg.

Jim Ruppel, director of customer relations, and Sherry Phelps, director of corporate employment, tell the story of a woman who frequently flew on Southwest but was disappointed with every aspect of the company's operation. In fact, she became known as the "Pen Pal" because after every flight she wrote in with a complaint. She didn't like the fact that the company didn't assign seats; she didn't like the absence of a first-class section; she didn't like not having a meal in flight; she didn't like Southwest's boarding procedure; she didn't like

> **Sending abusive customers to your best competitors is a great strategic action.**

the flight attendants' sporty uniforms and the casual atmosphere. And she hated peanuts! Her last letter, reciting a litany of complaints, momentarily stumped Southwest's customer-relations people.

Phelps explains: "Southwest prides itself on answering every letter that comes to the company and several employees tried to respond to this customer, patiently explaining why we do things the way we do them. [Our response] was quickly becoming a [large] volume until they bumped it up to Herb's desk, with a note: 'This one's yours.' In sixty seconds, Kelleher wrote back and said, 'Dear Mrs. Crabapple, We will miss you. Love, Herb.'"

Although there are many examples in organizations where the customer is right, there will always be examples where the customer is not right. In those examples, siding with your employees is the right thing to do. Sending abusive customers to your best competitors is a great strategic action. It also builds an incredibly loyal relationship between employees and management. As Gordon Bethune highlighted very carefully, customers constantly come and go, but your employees are with you day in and day out. Your ultimate responsibility, as a leader, is to them.

> "Your most unhappy customers are your greatest source of learning."
> **BILL GATES**

Strategy 76. Make your customer feel special

Ask people: "What are you looking for when you are served by others?" and responses will include:

- I want to be respected.
- I want someone to acknowledge me.
- I want someone to meet my needs.

- I want to quickly find what I'm looking for.
- I want someone to answer my questions.
- I want someone who serves me with a smile.
- I want someone to get me what I want—quickly.
- I want someone who appreciates my business.

When customers are served and these needs are adequately met, your organization can safely say that you have met your customers' needs.

I (Peter) once had the unfortunate experience of flying United Express and getting to the Santa Maria Airport in central California approximately forty minutes prior to my flight's departure. The lone ticket agent told me that I would not be able to obtain a boarding pass because I did not arrive one hour in advance of my flight. As she was leaving the desk to go to the tarmac and greet the arrival of the incoming flight, I shared with the ticket agent that I was unaware of the one-hour advance arrival. In response, she pulled out a counter pamphlet, circled the one-hour recommendation, handed it to me, and abandoned the counter. The flight left without me.

I was furious but smart enough to recognize that unless I wanted to drive from Santa Maria to San Diego, I had better be diplomatic in my negotiations. Two hours after my scheduled flight departed, the gate agent allowed me to board the next plane heading to Los Angeles. Once I arrived home, I sent an e-mail regarding my complaint to United Airlines that stated the following:

> If your goal is to close down the Santa Maria Operations and divert passengers to American Airlines out of San Luis Obispo, your ticket counter agents in Santa Maria are doing a great job.

Six weeks later, United Airlines "promptly" sent their response saying:

> Dear Mr. Stark:
> Thank you for your letter praising our employees at the Santa Maria Airport. We

are very proud of their dedication to our valued customers. Your comments are a
tribute to their professionalism, and I know they will appreciate you taking the
time from your busy schedule to write. I'm sending them a copy of your e-mail,
along with our thanks for an outstanding job. We appreciate this opportunity to
be of assistance and look forward to serving you.

I was dumbfounded. The same day, I sent a response to United
Airlines that stated:

Did anyone read my last e-mail? You are compounding the problem.

Seven days later, United Airlines responded stating:

Thank you for contacting us again. I apologize if my previous response gave you
the impression that I did not read your e-mail. While most e-mail communication is informal, I certainly respect your feelings on this issue as well. Your
feedback is well taken and important to us. We look forward to another opportunity to serve your travel needs.

Did I feel special? I felt so special I decided right then and there to
only utilize United Airlines as a last resort—when I have no other
options!

During this same time frame, I placed an order with Amazon.com.
Amazon immediately e-mailed me that the product I ordered was not
in stock. Because it was not, they would ship my product for free
when it was back in stock. I sent Amazon the following e-mail:

Thank you for informing me that my order will not be shipped today and that
the shipping is now free. I appreciate the great service

One hour and six minutes from my first e-mail contact, I received
the following response:

Thank you for writing to Amazon.com with your kind comments. We want to
provide service on a level that customers will remember, and it is always grati-

fying to know that we have succeeded. Thanks for taking the time to write to us. We look forward to filling your order and thank you for shopping at Amazon.com!

Best Regards,

Harjeev Mehta, Amazon.com Customer Service

Amazon, even in an electronic world, understands how to make customers feel special. The counter agent at United Airlines could have cared less how I felt, let alone whether I felt special. What is amazing is how many people have come up to us after our speeches and said, "You know … this was a great example. I have been served by both of these businesses and I have felt the difference."

It is pretty simple. If you want to provide extraordinary service and build your brand, make your customers feel special.

> "Being on par in terms of price and quality only gets you into the game. Service wins the game."
> **TONY ALESSANDRA**

PART FOUR

The Outcomes of Workplace Excellence

7 Priceless

There are so many things you can buy for your business. You can buy the best technology and equipment to support the needs of your employees, and fine furniture to furnish beautiful offices and snappy cubicles. You can purchase rewards to appropriately recognize your highest achievers. You can hire a concierge who runs errands for your employees, and a masseuse to relieve the stress of your work environment. You can even buy people by paying them a wage they cannot find anywhere else in the universe.

But no matter how hard you try, you cannot buy the six most signif icant outcomes from having an environment where your employees love to come to work and your customers love to do business.

What makes it so difficult for organizations to compete against a company that is in the Best-of-the-Best Benchmark is that the best have achieved these outcomes. No matter how hard you try, these outcomes cannot be bought. That is why these outcomes are priceless.

Priceless Outcome #1: Employees Feel They Are Treated Fairly

The Best-of-the-Best organizations understand that treating people fairly does not mean the same thing as treating people equally. If you treated everyone equally there would be no need to provide people with disabilities with preferential parking and special access to buildings. But, if you did not provide preferential parking and special access to the bathrooms in buildings, it would not be fair.

Customers understand the concept of fairness extremely well. That is why the frequent flier programs have worked so positively in building passenger loyalty with the airlines. When a grocery store prints out a $5 off coupon for the next shopping trip because you bought $250 of groceries during the previous month, the customer behind you does not say, "Hey, that's not fair."

Employees who work for Best-of-the-Best organizations share a lot with customers. They understand and appreciate being treated fairly, and they recognize that *fair* does not mean "equal." That is why the Best-of-the-Best organizations recognize and value the employees who provide innovation and tirelessly work to solve problems more than they value employees who just do their jobs.

For the same reasons, the Best-of-the-Best go out of their way to differentiate the rewards given to the top performers. Holding everyone accountable to clearly communicated performance standards helps to eliminate the feeling of favoritism. When all the questions in the employee opinion survey are compared between the two benchmarks, the question regarding favoritism has the widest spread, with the Best-of-the-Best exceeding the Overall Benchmark by 29.3 percentage points.

Recently, a CEO told us that he had a policy of not publicly recognizing employees for successful results because he felt it only served to upset the employees who received no recognition. Duh—it is supposed to! The CEO was right that some employees might be upset, but maybe stirring a little uneasiness into the rest of the workforce is not a bad thing. If you are fair in how you go about recognizing and rewarding the top performers maybe more people will say,

"Hey, I am also capable of producing extraordinary results." They might be motivated to raise their contributions to an even higher level.

When we interview employees in organizations where policies, procedures, and pay systems are not fair, most high performers ask the question, "Why should I go out of my way to work twelve hours a day when I am given the same raise as someone who comes to work late each day and struggles to contribute two hours of real work?" It is an excellent question.

Clearly, communicating performance standards and then holding people accountable to them helps to build an environment that is fair and absent of favoritism. Recognizing and rewarding the best performers sends a message that the system is fair but not equal. The data demonstrate that the Best-of-the-Best firmly root this concept in their cultures. They exceed the organizations in the Overall Benchmark by 14.9 percentage points in response to the statement, "At my company, I am treated fairly."

Priceless Outcome #2: Trust in Management and/or the Owners

Do your employees trust their manager or your management team? It is almost impossible to become a Best-of-the-Best organization when trust in senior or middle management, or even trust with the immediate supervisor, is not present.

Trust pays big dividends. A 2005 Watson Wyatt Worldwide study found that companies with high integrity (measured in employee opinion surveys of senior management's consistency, communication, and other trust-determining behaviors) generated financial returns that were twice those of companies with low integrity levels (*HR Magazine*, June 2006).

Unfortunately, trust is an elusive asset in organizations. The presence of trust is an outcome of how well your organization successfully implements The 10 Keys to Workplace Excellence. Our data tell us that a lack of trust in managers, especially senior managers, strongly influences an organization's ability to establish workplace excellence. For example, in response to the statement, "I trust the management team," the Best-of-the-Best exceed our Overall Benchmark by 16 percentage points.

The higher up you are on the management ladder, the harder it is for you to build a strong bond of trust with your employees because you have less time and opportunities to build one-on-one relationships. While 72.9% of the employees strongly agree or agree they trust the management team, even more (80.6%) of the employees trust their immediate supervisor.

Priceless Outcome #3: I Love My Job!

Are you one of the *lucky* people in this world who can honestly say, "I love my job"? We emphasize the word *lucky* because when you love your job, it does not seem like work. When you do not love what you do or where you do it, there is nothing harder than work.

We have interviewed hundreds of people who proudly say, "I love my job." The interviews revealed that four major features distinguished these people and their work environments.

First, engaged employees who love their jobs are competent in what they do and confident in how they do it. In other words, they are good at their jobs and they know it.

Second, these engaged employees enjoy variety in their work. They are not doing the same job over and over each day. One moment they are in a meeting with a major customer, the next, they are dealing with an employee concern. Then they work on an idea for a new product or service. Last, they spend some of their time returning voicemails and e-mails. Every day it is something different.

Third, these employees are empowered to make decisions and take actions to get their jobs accomplished.

Fourth, people who love their jobs feel challenged to accomplish their work. They must think in order to get their job done. Even though some of the people tell us they find it easy to do their jobs, they also tell us that not everyone is able to successfully do what they do.

People who love their jobs tend to believe that the work they are doing is important. Don Phillips, the superintendent of the nationally recognized Poway Unified School District, said it best when he stated, "We are spending our time on really significant work, and I think we are doing it well."

What is important to note is that very seldom does one of the employees who loves the job add, "And, I also love the money." Money will not buy you a love for your job. Some people like to say that enough money will at least allow you to not hate your job. We don't believe it. We have interviewed too many extremely well-paid people who hate their jobs and would rather be doing anything else.

When people feel competent and confident about jobs that provide them with challenge, empowerment, and variety, they will develop passion for and enjoy their jobs. Our data show that in response to the statement, "People at my company enjoy what they do," the Best-of-the-Best organizations exceed the Overall Benchmark by 15.8 percentage points.

Priceless Outcome #4: **Retention**

When companies fail to create workplace excellence and employees are not engaged, the best employees leave first. They can depart because they are the ones with the greatest number of viable options. Everyone who has ever worked with your finest employees, if given the option, would likely follow them to their next organization. Retention of your top employees becomes a major issue when your organization fails to establish a great working environment.

But your bigger retention problem involves the marginal or poor performers who are happy to stay. They will remain with your organization for a lifetime because they have very few options. Anyone who leaves your organization does not plan to take the marginal performers along. Unless you plan to change the marginal or poor performers' behaviors or share them with a competitor, these people are yours for life.

As we have seen, the Best-of-the-Best do a much better job at maintaining high performance standards in their organizations. Marginal employees usually do not last long. Poor and marginal employees best serve the Best-of-the-Best organizations by working for a competitor.

When responding to the following statement, "My company offers me the chance to have the kind of job I will want three years from now," Best-of-the-Best employees' ratings exceeded the ratings from employees in the Overall Benchmark by 15.1 percentage points.

Employees who feel valued and appreciated and are given the opportunity to do meaningful work, stay. Give employees some say in how their jobs are designed, managed, and measured and your chances are even higher that you will keep a loyal, engaged workforce.

Priceless Outcome #5: Employees Feel Valued

In the old days, mom and dad worked for one company their entire lives because loyalty to a boss and the employer was very important. In fact, if you held three or four different jobs in a period of ten years, you were labeled as a drifter. Even if our parents did not feel valued, loyalty was perceived as more important than switching jobs.

Today, if employees do not feel their contributions are valued, they are likely to leave, either physically or mentally.

Successfully implementing The 10 Keys to Workplace Excellence is essential to build an environment where employees feel valued. Communicating the organization's vision and expectations for performance helps to set up employees for success. Providing training and growth and learning opportunities *directly* tells employees that they are assets worth the investment. Recognizing employees for their contributions *directly* lets employees know they are valued. The impact of feeling valued is that employees feel a stronger bond or connection with their manager and the company.

It does not matter if you are in a personal or business relationship. When you feel valued, you are much more willing to go out of your way and supply the discretionary effort to make your counterpart successful and happy. Being an employer of first choice, with fully engaged employees, is a great way to work.

Priceless Outcome #6: Positive **Reputation for Workplace Excellence**

There are only two types of reputations: good and bad.

Your organization's success depends on your positive reputation for an environment where your employees love to come to work and your customers love to do business. When you establish a positive reputation for workplace excellence, people will be attracted to you as an employer, which will make it easier to attract and retain the top talent in the industry. Starbucks, which provides benefits to part-time employees who work 240 hours a quarter, has earned this positive reputation because it values and invests in its employees.

Would you like to see these priceless outcomes alive in your workplace? Most managers would say yes. Great leaders would add that it is difficult to effectively run an organization without these outcomes in place. These leaders understand that these outcomes are the competitive weapons the Best-of-the-Best organizations use to win the talent wars and capture profitable market share.

There are some leaders who are so focused on *bottom line results* that they don't think much about the people in their organizations. There are other leaders who are so concerned about the *people* that they make bad decisions that ultimately undermine the success of their organizations.

The ten keys described in chapter two, along with the seventy-six strategies described in chapter six, are used by great leaders to create an environment where employees love to come to work and customers love to do business. The data emphasize the significant difference between the Best-of-the-Best organizations, and the organizations represented in the Overall Benchmark. The results irrefutably show every leader that it is possible to be focused on both *results and people*.

We'd be the first to acknowledge that creating workplace excellence leading to employee engagement is not easy. But, there is great news. Learning from those leaders in the Best-of-the-Best organizations and taking action will lead to your long-term success. You, too, can experience the benefits and excitement of working with an engaged work-force. Don't wait for the CEO, Human Resource Department, or for your boss to tell you to take action. No one else can do it. Creating an engaged workforce starts with you!

TIP

Wondering what an Employee Opinion Survey can do for your organization? Go to www.peterstark.com, and enter the word ENGAGE in the Tip Box.

ACKNOWLEDGMENTS

The Peter Barron Stark Companies Team

This book could not be a reality if it were not for the valiant efforts of our team. We are blessed to work with some of the most dedicated and talented people in the world. For over fifteen years, Dusty Tockstein and Kimberly Juntunen have helped our clients by flawlessly administering the engagement surveys and then analyzing the data to present the findings in a meaningful way. Dusty and Kimberly are constantly looking for ways to improve the survey process and provide meaningful data and recommendations to our clients. Patti McCord, our client services manager, has constantly kept this project moving forward. From adding great ideas to make the content even more meaningful, to coordinating the editors and designers who have brought life to this book, Patti has brought enthusiasm and vision at the most important times—especially when Jane or I felt the frustrations that are inherent in writing a book. Marilyn, Dawn, and Diane, our assistants: thank you for everything you do to keep our lives in order. Without your attention to details and ensuring that each one of our presentations, seminars, or speeches is a "10," we would not have had the time to write this book.

Our Editorial and Design Team

We gratefully acknowledge the efforts of our editorial team. Pat Ryan took our original writings and helped us to organize our thoughts and formulate the book. From there, Susan Suffes, who is a master editorial architect, was invaluable in ensuring that our writing was "tight" and that what we were communicating was stated in the most effective manner. Finally, Jessica Swift went through our final manuscript with a fine-tooth comb to ensure that all the i's were dotted and the t's were crossed. Our designer, Debbie Glasserman, had a compelling positive vision for both the layout and cover. We had a vision for a design that was fresh and exciting and with Debbie's design expertise, she brought our vision to life. As authors, we have one strength—we can put our thoughts on paper. Without the help of this team, the end result would not have the same impact.

Our Clients

Without our clients who have partnered with our firm and implemented our recommendations, we would not have witnessed first-hand the positive results that are achieved when great leaders have the determination to drive results combined with the vision to create an organization where employees love coming to work. You are our heroes and we are so grateful for the opportunity to work with you.

The following clients graciously gave us feedback, providing inspiration so this book would be all we dreamed it would be and to help leaders build even stronger organizations. We are indebted to you for your time and expertise.

Jim Konrath	Accredited Home Lenders
Anthony Robbins	Anthony Robbins Companies
Bruce Hendricks	Bank of Nevada
Mitch Ardantz	Bonita Packing Co./Betteravia Farms
Lori Poole	California Bank & Trust
Gail Sullivan	City of Escondido

Lowell Billings	Chula Vista Elementary School District
Harry Paul	coauthor, *Fish! and Instant Turnaround!*
Parker Cann	Columbia Credit Union
Bob Adams	Crain Communications
Timothy Fennell	Del Mar Fairgrounds/Racetrack
Jim Daues	Farmers Insurance
Doran Barnes	Foothill Transit
Kevin Freiberg	freibergs.com
Sharon Owen	Gibson, Dunn & Crutcher
Jon Peters	The Institute for Management Studies
Hemi Zucker	j2 Global Communications
Ken Blanchard	The Ken Blanchard Companies
Sadie Stern	LG Electronics
Jack Farnan	Mitchell International
Mike Maslak	North Island Credit Union
Terry Paulson, PhD	Paulson and Associates
Pete Wong	Phoenix Suns–U.S. Airways Center
Don Phillips	Poway Unified School District
Michael Easley	Powder River Energy Corporation
Pam Smith	San Diego County Health & Human Service
Paul Barnes	SheaHomes San Diego Division
Ruby Randall	Vistage
Garry Ridge	WD-40 Company
Chris Folz	Wells Fargo
Kathleen Vaughan	Wells Fargo & Company

SEVEN WAYS TO ENGAGE!

1. Engage Your Employees with an Employee Opinion Survey

We've surveyed nearly 100,000 employees and managers around the world and can guide you through the process to make it simple and easy for you. Then we'll deliver a customized report broken down by department to provide you with an overall picture of the areas where your organization is effective and those where there are opportunities for improvement. We specialize in building organizations where employees love to come to work!

2. Engage Your Employees with Our Training Programs Addressing:

- Surviving and Thriving During Times of Change
- Communication Skills
- Presentation Skills
- Dealing with Difficult Customers
- Extraordinary Customer Service
- Negotiation and Persuasion Training

3. Engage Your Customers with a Customer Service/Satisfaction Survey

We will work with you to create, administer, and process a survey that will determine the areas of your organization that are doing well and those that need to be improved or refined. After the initial survey process is complete, we use our expertise to interpret the results and make specific recommendations to help strengthen your organization.

4. Engage Your Leaders with Our Training Programs Addressing:

- Leadership
- Relationship Strategies—Dealing with Different Types of People
- Communication Skills
- Performance Management
- Delivering Difficult Feedback to Increase Performance

- Motivating Your Team ... Without Money
- Conflict Resolution
- Leading Organizational Change
- Team Building

5. Engage Your Leaders with a Leadership Development Assessment (360° Evaluation)

Our Leadership Development Assessment (LDA) is an organizational tool for helping all managers become more effective by increasing their self-awareness and self-understanding. The LDA works on the principle of multilevel feedback and provides a comparative profile of the managers' leadership skills, as seen by others and themselves. This feedback provides a personal portrait of each manager's leadership role. Our consultants work with the managers to create customized recommendations and a proposed Action Plan to help them become the leaders they want to be.

6. Engage Your Leaders with Our Executive Coaching Program

We provide a customized plan designed to help leaders reach their potential. Leaders who have completed this program say they have discovered their purpose and passion and developed the necessary skills to build strong relationships throughout the organization, coupled with a renewed confidence for leading their teams to success.

7. Engage Your Executive Team Through:

- Organizational Assessments
- Meeting Facilitation
- Strategic Planning
- Team Building

For more information about Customer Service/Satisfaction Surveys and Employee Opinion Surveys, visit www.employeeopinionsurveys.com. To find out more about employee engagement and to see program descriptions, visit www.peterstark.com.